Numerous national polls, including my own survey of paranormal occurrences, agree with my supposition that the walls that separate us from the Shadow World are very thin. For example:

- The April 20, 1998 issue of *USA Today* states that belief in the Beyond has grown sharply since the 1970s. In 1998, according to recent statistics, fifty-two percent of adult Americans believed in spirit contact.
- The December 1996 issue of *George*, a magazine of political commentary, stated in their survey of "What Does America Believe?" that thirty-nine percent of those polled believed in ghosts and haunted houses.
- *Better Homes and Gardens* surveyed more than 80,000 of its readers and discovered that 89 percent believed in life after death, 30 percent had perceived an astral (spirit) realm, and 13 percent accepted the possibility of spirit communication with the living.

It does seem that just as we are but one species of human inhabiting the material world with our multitude of physical variations, so, too, might the non-material Shadow World include a host of entities with a multitude of expressions and purposes. . . .

SHADOW WORLD

Brad Steiger

A SIGNET VISIONS BOOK

Although the events and experiences recounted
in this book are true and happened to real people,
the names of most individuals have been
changed to protect their privacy.

SIGNET
Published by New American Library, a division of
Penguin Putnam Inc., 375 Hudson Street,
New York, New York 10014, U.S.A.
Penguin Books Ltd, 27 Wrights Lane,
London W8 5TZ, England
Penguin Books Australia Ltd,
Ringwood, Victoria, Australia
Penguin Books Canada Ltd, 10 Alcorn Avenue,
Toronto, Ontario, Canada M4V 3B2
Penguin Books (N.Z.) Ltd, 182–190 Wairau Road,
Auckland 10, New Zealand

Penguin Books Ltd, Registered Offices:
Harmondsworth, Middlesex, England

First published by Signet, an imprint of New American Library,
a division of Penguin Putnam Inc.

First Printing, April 2000
10 9 8 7 6 5 4 3 2 1

Contents

CHAPTER ONE

Welcome to Shadow World

Whenever I appear on Jeff Rense's "Sightings on Radio," which is broadcast to dozens of radio stations across the nation, or on Art Bell's "Coast to Coast," a five-hour radio event that is heard by sixteen million listeners on over four hundred affiliates, large numbers of their listening audiences call in to seek my counsel regarding their haunted homes and to ask how best to proceed with the spirit energies that have made their lives incredibly complicated—and sometimes incredibly frightening. During each of my appearances on these and other radio shows on which I regularly appear, we receive hundreds of calls, faxes, and emails. In addition, I often receive as many as eight hundred letters after each one of these coast-to-coast, all-night explorations of ghostly goings-on.

The men and women who call, fax, email, or write come from all walks of life and include a remarkable range of professions and occupations, from law enforcement officers to members of the clergy, from attorneys to military personnel. Haunting phenomena hold no respect for social position, bank accounts, rank, or privilege.

Based on the number of cries for help that I receive from these haunted listeners, it would surely seem that there are thousands of people who have met the eerie inhabitants of Shadow World. Here are only a few samples from recent callers:

- A trailer park is terrorized by the hostile spirit of a man who hanged himself in his mobile home. The manifestations have become so frightening that several residents of the park suffer heart attacks after their encounters with the physically aggressive spirit.
- The ghosts of long-dead children are blamed for the eerie death of a construction worker who was helping to tear down an old school building.
- A man has a near-death experience and returns with a disruptive spirit who had been trapped between dimensions.
- A house is possessed with animal spirits that seem determined to make a couple's five-year-old child their permanent playmate.
- A small town of six hundred inhabitants is haunted by the ghost of a young woman who died of pneumonia before her wedding day in 1914.

- A man in his fifties has been continually haunted by mysterious presences ever since he disturbed an artifact in sacred ground when he was a boy of seventeen.

A SHADOW WORLD EXISTS ALL AROUND US

Since the late 1950s, I have been invited to private homes, office buildings, dormitories, hospitals, and sacred tribal areas to investigate the manifestations of real ghosts, restless spirits, and haunted minds. I have found that there is a Shadow World that exists all around us, and when it impinges upon our ordinary plane of shared reality this dark dimension is sometimes frightening, occasionally menacing, but always worthy of cautious exploration.

I have conducted my explorations of the Shadow World in forty-six states, a number of Canadian provinces, and in such foreign countries as Egypt, Israel, Jordan, and Peru.

I have seen experienced police officers turn tail and run when confronted by *something* that was most certainly not covered in their training manuals.

I have witnessed materializations of spirit entities, heard spectral voices, felt ghostly touches on my person—and once, in a home in which five violent murders had occurred, I was even lifted into the air by a nasty being that I had angered. But perhaps nothing was quite so unsettling as a haunting in my own home.

HOME IS WHERE THE HAUNT IS

They were auctioning off the last of the farm equipment when a man I recognized as the local fire chief approached me.

"Man, did you ever get a good buy," he said, smiling broadly as he gestured toward the magnificent old farmhouse. "Especially you, of all people. It's just perfect for you."

Having just learned that he was a cousin of the previous owner, I replied somewhat cautiously. "I think I paid a reasonable price for the house, the outbuildings, and the acreage."

"I'm not talking about what you paid for the place," he said, laughing loud enough to direct the attention of several people away from the auctioneer and toward us. "I meant you really got a bonus. You write about ghosts and chase after spooky things all over the country. Well, my friend, you just bought yourself a genuine haunted house! We buried Grandpa's body five years ago, but his ghost has never moved out of the house."

My family and I soon found out that the man was not joking.

The eerie manifestations began shortly after we had moved in during the summer of 1973, and they did not abate for several months. The very presence of my wife, four children, and myself seemed to be an affront to the invisible force that dwelt within the old farmhouse, and it tried every frightening method that it could devise to drive us out.

In retrospect, I am certain that I must have really set the haunting into maximum motion by my efforts to modernize the place. My own vivid childhood memories included the lighting of kerosene lamps, rushing to outdoor toilets on cold winter nights, and the daily task of carrying drinking water from the well to the kitchen, and I had no desire to return to those rugged days of yesteryear—nor did I think my wife and children wished to adopt a rustic lifestyle circa 1930.

While I was in the process of drilling a well and installing indoor plumbing, modern toilets, and electrical appliances, neighbors informed me that the old patriarch had never believed in such newfangled inventions. He considered them to be devices of sinful indulgence, and he was dead set against them. He forbade any of his children, including the daughter from whom I had bought the place, to install such modern conveniences.

I Receive a Rousing Other-Worldly Welcome

Rightfully so, I suppose, I was the first member of the family to be the intended victim of a psychic barrage of haunting manifestations terrifyingly designed to drive me out of the house.

I was alone one morning when I heard a thunderous explosion in the basement. Then, while I was investigating the basement area, the attic sounded as if lightning had struck the rafters.

By the time that I had run up three flights of stairs to the attic, the entire house was alive with loud thumps, bumps, and thudding footsteps running from room to room.

I was more intrigued and fascinated than I was frightened. By this time in my career, I had already devoted twenty years to psychical research, and I had investigated numerous haunted houses, observed a vast array of paranormal phenomena, and written nearly thirty books on the unknown and the unexplained.

Then, too, I grew up in a house that harbored a fairly large variety of other-worldly manifestations, so I was probably no more than three years old when I saw my first ghostly visitors. But while the appearance of spectral entities, the sounds of measured footsteps, and the infrequent psychokinetic displays in my childhood home were never all that disturbing, the manifestations in the farmhouse seemed deliberately produced to frighten, perhaps even to threaten.

I remained calm and dealt directly with the negative energy, slowly dissipating its force until all was quiet in the house. I chose not to mention the incident to my wife or the children. No use upsetting them. It was all over.

Wrong!

The energy of the haunting phenomena soon returned with renewed power and wreaked havoc on us for many months to come. It had deceptively appeared to retreat so that it might regroup and attack each of us one by one. Furious poundings drummed relentlessly on the walls, ceilings, doors, and windows.

Mysterious lights appeared both inside and outside of the house. Footsteps thundered up and down the stairs. Doors opened and closed of their own volition.

We had entered a Shadow World from which it seemed there was no easy exit. And then, after a time, perhaps because we stubbornly remained in the house, the energy dissipated.

Julie, the youngest child and the most vulnerable family member, received the brunt of the haunting and was the victim of its cruelest phenomena. For a time, I feared that she might be traumatized by her frightening personal experiences.

Interestingly, however, when Julie and I were recently discussing the terrible events of nearly twenty-seven years ago, I discovered that she has now chosen to place a positive interpretation on her childhood experiences in a haunted house.

"You know, Dad," she said, "even though those days were some of the most horrible of my life, the positive aspect of it all is that I also experienced direct proof that there really is *something* within us that survives physical death."

To experience a haunting, to see a ghost, Julie decided, is to receive proof that life goes on beyond the grave.

WHY WE ARE ATTRACTED TO STORIES OF HAUNTINGS

I think that Julie may really have touched on the basic reason why human beings have always loved ghost stories and tales of haunted houses. Whether one hears them around campfires or views them at the cineplex, stories of hauntings, no matter how frightening, are at the same time reassuring to the innermost reaches of the human psyche.

Accounts of ghostly manifestations, regardless of how terrifying they may be, demonstrate that life exists in more than one dimension of reality. Reports of restless spirits, although horrifying, suggest that we may all be multidimensional beings and that there is some aspect of the human mind-body-soul construct that survives physical death.

From 1958 to 1989, I actively sought out and investigated dozens of haunted houses, places, and people. Since that time, hauntings have come to my attention through requests for assistance in dealing with troubled dwellings, or I have been drawn into spiritually charged areas during my travels with my wife, Sherry, who is an ordained Protestant minister and who has many psychic abilities and spiritual gifts.

AN EERIE ENCOUNTER IN A BED-AND-BREAKFAST INN

A few years ago when Sherry and I were scheduled to lecture in Bellingham, Washington, our friend and sponsor, Benjamin Smith, suggested that we stay in a sprawling, picturesque mansion that had been converted into a bed-and-breakfast establishment by its present owners. Each of the guest bedrooms had been styled to depict a different country, culture, or time period, and we chose an elegant Victorian on the third floor.

Sherry awakened in the night, surprised to see me out of bed. She could clearly see a shadowy male figure of my general size and build standing at the window with his back to her. As she watched, he walked away from the window and crossed the room to take a seat in one of the large, overstuffed chairs near the door. She had the strong impression that I was ill or restlessly anxious.

"Honey," she whispered. "Are you all right? Are you nervous about tomorrow's lecture? What is wrong? What are you doing?"

My muffled voice rising from the pillow beneath the mound of blankets beside her gave Sherry a start she is not likely to forget. "*I'm* trying to sleep," I mumbled in answer to her queries. "What are *you* doing?"

Before her astonished eyes, the shadowy form of the man—who most certainly was not her husband—vanished.

After she had related her account of the mysterious disappearing male figure, we managed to fall back to sleep.

But this was not to be the last of Sherry's ghostly encounters during our overnight stay in the majestic old mansion.

Sometime before dawn, she felt what she believed to be my hand comfortingly taking one of her own and squeezing it lovingly and reassuringly. However, as she became more aware of the size and the feel of the hand, she realized that it was far too small to be mine.

Opening her eyes, she clearly perceived that it was a baby's hand that was clutching her own. Attached to the tiny hand was an arm, *but no body.*

At breakfast the next morning, we learned that a woman and her infant son had died in that bedroom during childbirth over thirty years ago. The distraught husband had spent the night anxiously pacing the floor, praying that his restless vigil might deliver them from the Angel of Death. According to the owners of the mansion, we were not the first guests who had witnessed the ghostly enactment of the domestic tragedy.

NATIONAL SURVEYS REVEAL MILLIONS BELIEVE IN GHOSTS

Numerous national polls, including our own survey of paranormal occurrences, agree with my supposition that the walls that separate us from Shadow World are very thin:

- The "USA Snapshots" feature in the April 20, 1998, issue of *USA Today* states that belief in the Beyond has grown sharply since the 1970s. In 1976, only 12 percent of adults polled believed in the possibility of encounters with the dead achieved through mediumship or haunting phenomena. In 1998, according to recent statistics, 52 percent of adult Americans believe in spirit contact.
- The December 1996 issue of *George*, a monthly magazine of political commentary, stated in their survey of "What Does America Believe?" that 39 percent of those polled believed in ghosts and haunted houses.
- In 1994, Jeffrey S. Levin, an associate professor at Eastern Virginia Medical School, Norfolk, Virginia, analyzed a national sociological survey conducted by the National Opinion Research Center, University of Chicago, and found that two-thirds of Americans said that they had at least one mystical experience. Of that vast number of experiencers 39.9 percent claimed that they had an encounter with a ghost or had achieved contact with the spirit of a deceased person.
- In the January/February 1987 issue of *American Health*, Father Andrew Greeley, a Roman Catholic priest with a doctorate in sociology, released data collected by colleagues at the University of

Chicago and the University of Arizona in Tucson that revealed that 42 percent of the adult population in the United States believe that they have interacted with spirits of the dead. Additionally, 73 percent believe in life after death and 74 percent expect to be reunited with their loved ones after death.

- In the fall of 1988, *Better Homes and Gardens* surveyed more than 80,000 of its readers and, among other findings, discovered that 89 percent believed in life after death, 30 percent perceived of an astral (spirit) realm, and 13 percent accept the possibility of spirit communication with the living.

- From our own *Steiger Questionnaire of Paranormal, Mystical, and UFO Experiences*, a survey process that we began in 1967, we have accumulated data that indicate that among those men and women who have responded to our books and to our media appearances and who have an interest in exploring the unknown or who may have a belief in supernatural manifestations, 48 percent are convinced that they have seen a ghost; 42 percent have perceived the spirit of a departed one; and 61 percent state that they have encountered spirit entities in "haunted" places.

IDENTIFYING THE SPIRIT INHABITANTS OF SHADOW WORLD

When one thinks of a haunted house, one typically envisions darkened corridors that echo each night with the moans and groans of the ghost of someone who once dwelt therein and who now makes occasional terrifying appearances to the present inhabitants. As a result of my forty-two years of investigation and research, however, I have found that the traditional haunting scenario is but one of many types of frightening phenomena created by a host of spirit beings who live in the Shadow World. What is more, a good many inhabitants of Shadow World may have absolutely nothing to do with spirits of the dead or the question of life after death. Some entities appear to be multidimensional beings, intelligences that enter our dimension of reality for purposes that may be beyond our capacity to imagine. Some may be benign, perhaps seeking to bring us higher awareness of the complex universe in which we reside. Others seem to be cosmic tricksters and troublemakers bent on mischief. And, unfortunately, there are some beings who do not appear to have our best interests at heart—in fact, they do not even seem to like us. They may have entered our world with the intention of possessing our bodies or capturing our souls.

Among the spirits and multidimensional beings that I have isolated in my research are the following:

Spirits of the Dead

The classic, traditional haunting manifestations generally are caused by earthbound spirits of deceased humans who have been unable to quit their attachment to the people, places, or things of the physical world and have not yet progressed into the Light of a higher spiritual dimension.

Poltergeists

Perhaps the most disruptive and unsettling kind of hauntings are those in which the psyche of a living human (usually an adolescent or someone undergoing psychic upheaval or the stresses of a severe psychological adjustment) expresses its unconscious aggression toward others in dramatic psychokinetic (mind over matter) displays: overturning furniture, making objects airborne. When poltergeist phenomena interact with the haunting manifestation that may already exist in a home, one must deal with a cosmic carnival of terror.

Phantoms

Ghostly apparitions that have been seen by many people over many years may literally begin to take on independent existences of their own, thus becoming psychic marionettes, responding to the fears and expectations of their human audiences. Almost every community in the nation has its traditional phantom, such as a Phantom Nun that haunts the ruins of a convent, a Phantom Horseman that guards an old bridge, a Phantom Hound that stands watch over a graveyard.

Animal Spirits

While many religions declare that only humans have souls, countless pet owners argue that animals also have a spiritual essence that may remain attached to certain people and places after physical death. So many individuals have shared extremely beautiful and inspirational accounts of devoted pets maintaining their loving presence from the Other Side that it seems to me that we must be prepared to grant credence to these personal testimonies. While most animal spirits appear to be benign, some defend their territory with the same ferociousness that they exhibited while in their physical bodies.

Nature Spirits

Whether you call these spirit beings devas, fairies, or elves, they have made themselves known to humans for centuries and very often provide exceedingly lively and frightening haunting phenomena. While the activities of most nature spirits are mischievous rather than malignant, many individuals have learned to their great regret that it is not wise to violate certain areas that were held sacred by the aboriginal inhabitants—and it is never a good idea to step inside a fairy circle.

Deiform Spirits

These beings may be a variation of nature spirits, but ancient people considered such entities as gods and goddesses, worshipping them, making sacrifices to them, and channeling messages from them. When Deiform Spirits physically manifest, they appear as majestic, archetypal, godlike beings. Whatever these entities may truly be, one finds them around old ruins and ancient burial grounds, as well as archaeological digs and excavations. They are reservoirs of great power and demand respect, and they can become extremely violent and vengeful if slighted or insulted.

Spirit Residue

Many so-called haunted places, perhaps the majority, contain no spirits or multidimensional beings, but merely the psychic residue left by powerful human emotions—such as hate, fear, pain—that have been somehow impressed into the natural environment and may be glimpsed by the psychically sensitive as if they were images on a strip of motion picture film that keeps being run through a projector again and again.

Spirit Parasites

The nastiest beings in Shadow World are the Spirit Parasites, entities that are especially dominant in places where murders or other acts of violence have been perpetrated. These entities can accumulate to make any house a repository of evil. Hideous and grotesque in appearance, they most often manifest as reptilian-type entities. Quite likely, Spirit Parasites are the traditional "demons" encountered throughout human history. They are also capable of possessing unaware or vulnerable humans.

Spirit Mimics

I sometimes refer to Spirit Mimics as the "In-between Beings," since they often pose as ordinary men and women in order to accomplish goals that remain difficult to ascertain from our human perspective.

I found a good description of these beings in a book by British author Thurston Hopkins, who, in his world travels, encountered the supernatural in its many guises. He, too, came to recognize a kind of spirit that appears to occupy a spiritual "no-man's land," and he describes them in this way:

"They are creatures who have strayed from some unknown region of haunted woods and perilous wilds. They dress like us; pretend they belong to mankind and profess to keep our laws and code of morals. But in their presence we are always aware that they are phantoms and that all their ideas and actions are out of key with the general pitch and tone of normal life." [*Adventures with Phantoms*, Quality Press, London, 1946.]

We must be open to the possibility that all of the above entities are really manifestations of a single source phenomenon that chooses to represent itself in a manner individual and meaningful to each particular witness of haunting phenomena. But it does seem that just as we are but one species of human inhabiting the material world with our multitude of physical variations, so, too, might the nonmaterial Shadow World include a host of entities with a multitude of expressions and purposes. In the next chapter we shall encounter specific examples of those beings who represent themselves as spirits of the dead, both benign and malicious.

CHAPTER TWO

*Contact with Spirits of
the Dead*

Over the past forty years of my research into the ghostly inhabitants of Shadow World, some of the men and women with whom I have spoken believed that their deceased loved ones have become their guardian angels. Certain theologians will argue that point, stating firmly that the heavenly angels are an ethereal species quite apart from humankind. According to most orthodox religious teachings, the angels were created by the Supreme Being to be cosmic citizens long before He shaped humans out of the clay of Earth.

James Mohr of Dallas will dispute that conventional angelic analysis. In his opinion, his deceased grandmother is his guardian angel—and she came back from the Other Side to save his life.

His Grandmother Is His Guardian Angel

"I was driving a rented truck, moving from Omaha to Dallas," Mohr told me. "My wife was following with the kids in our van about a day or so behind. I had gone on ahead to meet her two brothers at our new home, and the plan was that we could get the furniture unloaded before she and the kids arrived to complete our moving-in. I was getting low on gas—and very sleepy—when I saw a small gas station and diner up ahead. I planned to pull over and fill up with gas and get some coffee and a sandwich when I got a whiff of something very familiar and very out of place. I was clearly and distinctly smelling Gram's lavender-scented powder. I had smelled it on her since I was a little kid. I would know it anywhere."

The recognition of the familiar scent brought James Mohr a clear materialization of Grandmother Mohr, who had been dead for nearly ten years. "As solidly as I see you now, Brad," Mohr said, "I saw Gram sitting opposite me in the cab of the truck. 'Jimmy,' she said, 'you just keep on driving to the next gas station. You don't want to go in that place up ahead. Stay clear of it, my little man. Something very bad is about to happen there very, very soon.'"

Mohr said that he didn't have to think twice about the admonition from the spirit of his grandmother. "She smiled at me, said she loved me and would watch over me until I walked in Heaven with her, then she disappeared. I didn't intellectualize that I had been driving too long and was hallucinating. It was just too damn real. I knew it had been Gram. First there was the smell of that lavender powder of hers, and then she called me 'little man.' Even after I got to be over six feet, she still always called me little man. I put the pedal to the metal and kept driving right on by the gas station and diner."

Late the next afternoon, just before he arrived in Dallas, he was having lunch in a restaurant outside the city when he saw a segment on the television newscast that showed the very traveler's oasis at which he would have stopped the night before. The diner had been robbed, and the savage thieves had brutally murdered the cook, the waitress, and two customers in order to leave no witnesses.

"The time of the awful murders checked with the exact time that I would have pulled into the gas station and diner," Mohr said. "If Gram's ghost had not appeared and told me not to stop but to keep on going, I would have been another murdered customer at the counter. I couldn't ask for a better guardian angel than Gram. We were very close when she was on Earth, and I guess we're even closer now that she's in Heaven."

She Met Her Spirit Guide on the Other Side

Diane Ching of Arizona said that she met her spirit guide, her great-uncle Chang Yun, on the Other Side when she nearly died during the crash of a small airplane in which she was the passenger.

"My friend Aaron had just received his pilot's license, and he wanted to show off to me," Diane said. "I had a bad feeling, a premonition, that I should not go with him that afternoon, but I wanted to show my confidence in his abilities. Next time, I will listen to my inner voice."

Diane Ching underwent a classic near-death experience. She saw herself moving down a dark tunnel toward a speck of light that grew larger as she drew nearer. "I was aware of an entity, a kind of guide, near to me as I moved closer to the light. And then, suddenly, I was standing on a small footbridge that stretched over a fish pond in a beautiful garden."

Slowly she became aware of people moving around her. "They all seemed very friendly, and they were smiling and welcoming me. They were people of all ethnic groups—white, black, yellow, red, brown—every hue of humanity, and they all seemed delighted to see me."

Just as Diane was growing accustomed to the concept of her death, a tall Chinese gentleman stepped forward and told her that her stay would be very brief. "He was very imposing, but in a gentle way," she remembered. "I remember that he had a beard, the kind that traditional wise men wear. He came closer to me and held out his arms so that I might embrace him. In a soft, yet commanding voice, he informed me that he would always be near me and watch over me. Then he asked me to look closer at the lovely goldfish swimming in the pond. One very large fish caught my attention, and as I watched its supple and graceful movements, it began to swim in circles. The next thing I knew, I was waking up in a hospital."

Diane Ching was in for a hospital stay of nearly two weeks and a period of convalescence in her parents' home. "I was not married at that time," she explained. "I was, in fact, only two months out of college and had not yet found a steady job. My parents were kind enough to extend their love and care to me as they had when I was a child."

One day, to pass the hours, Diane's mother brought down a number of old family scrapbooks. "As we paged through the photographs, I felt as if we were gazing at the pictorial history of our family's acculturation into American society. And then I felt a little shiver of recognition when I saw a photograph of the distinguished Chinese gentleman who had embraced me in the lovely garden on the Other Side. In the picture, he stood with two little boys, one I recognized as Father. 'Ah,' Mother said, 'why, that is your grandfather's brother, your great-uncle Chang Yun. He was a very wise and good man, known widely for many acts of kindness. He died very young, when he was not yet forty, trying to rescue a small girl who was drowning. I barely knew him. I was only six or seven when he died.'"

Diane told her mother of her near-death experience and her visit to the gardens of paradise where she had met Chang Yun. "'He embraced me, Mother, and said that he would always watch over me.' Mother got tears in her eyes and told me with great emotion in her voice that I could not have a better guiding spirit to look after me."

His Spirit Came Home for Christmas

In August of 1991, Louise Horton wrote to tell me an inspirational story of how the spirit of her recently deceased son came home for one last Christmas celebration with his family.

The Horton family buried Rick, a husband and father, on December 4, 1977. An automobile accident while on a business trip had taken him from his wife, Melba, his three young children, and his loving parents, Louise and Charles. In her account of the experience, Louise wrote:

> Rick would have been thirty-eight years old the day before Christmas, and in spite of the heavy cloud of grief that hung over all of us, Charlie and I decided that we would do everything that we could to make the remainder of the Christmas holiday just as happy as possible. We knew in our hearts that Rick would have wanted it that way.

Louise and Charles set about decorating the house inside and out, just as they had done every Christmas since Rick was a small boy. They made certain that Melba and the kids knew that they were to come over on Christmas Eve for a big turkey dinner and the opening of their presents around the festive Christmas tree. Then they would stay overnight, and all the Hortons would go to church as a family on Christmas Day. Everything would be just as it would have been if Rick had not been taken from them.

As Louise and Charles were assembling the same miniature manger scene that they had placed on the fireplace mantel ever since Rick was seven years old, it came to Louise to fashion a small home altar to commemorate their son's memory.

We bought a terrarium to honor Rick's love of plants and nature. Charlie filled a tall, purple-tinted urn with scented water. Around Rick's picture, we placed a tall red candle in a bright green holder and a number of Christmas tree ornaments to add the touch of holiday color that he had always loved so very much. Just off to the left side, we placed a small incense burner in which we lighted cones of sandalwood incense two or three times a day.

Just a few days before Christmas, Charles solemnly lighted the tall red candle in the altar, and Louise lay before it a Bible open to the Christmas story in St. Matthew. Both of them offered silent prayers toward the same unspoken request—that they somehow be given a sign that Rick's spirit was a happy one.

Louise remembers that she began to cry softly, then lowered her head against her husband's shoulder. "Don't cry, Mom," he comforted her, taking one of her hands in his own. "If there is any way between heaven and earth for Rick to make contact with us, you know that he will find it."

Louise smiled, recalling how Charles had tried to tame their son's assertive personality when Rick was a boy, but had come to admire his aggressiveness. Rick had the knack of knowing when to turn on the charm and when to push for what he wanted. He had used this balance of talents successfully through high school, college, and the business world. If only he hadn't been taken from his family when he was so young.

"You know, sweetheart," Charles said, chuckling at the flow of memories, "there wasn't anything on this whole planet that that boy couldn't figure out. He would just keep at any problem until he had it figured out. If there is a way to bring us a message, you know he will do it. I'll bet at this very minute he's probably lecturing a bunch of angels on how they could do their jobs more efficiently."

On Christmas Eve, Louise was up early to begin to prepare a hearty meal for the family. Melba and the children would arrive around five o'clock for an early dinner. Everyone would have to help clean up the dishes and the kitchen, then it would be time to open the presents under the tree. Melba and the children arrived a bit early, just a little after four.

Sometimes I get a bit nervous and jumpy when I feel that I am pressured. I knew the kids would start snooping around the presents and be getting into things they shouldn't. Charlie was reading the evening paper, so I knew that he wouldn't be doing much policing of his grandkids. Melba asked if she could help fill the relish trays and so forth, but I'm fussy about finishing things that I start.

So what I am saying is that *normally* the music coming from the radio wouldn't have bothered me, but right then, it was getting on my nerves. I waited to speak until I knew that I was calm enough not to shout, then I said to Charlie, "I love Christmas carols as much as the next person, but could we do without them for a little while?"

Louise recalls that Charles gave her one of his famous blank looks. "What do you mean, Mom? What Christmas carols?"

She took his question to signal resistance to her subtle request to turn off the radio. Her voice rose a bit louder, "At least until I finish preparing dinner, *please* shut off the radio."

"Louise, honey," her husband said quietly, "there is no radio or television set or record player on in this house at this time."

And then they all began to pay attention to the music that was filtering through the house. It was a lovely haunting melody, strangely familiar, yet none of them could identify it. As Louise remembered,

We all agreed that it certainly sounded Christmaslike, but none of us could tell exactly what hymn or popular holiday song it might be. We looked everywhere for the source of the beautiful melody. We kept hearing that there was sometimes

27

a chorus of voices with the music that sounded like angels singing. Charles even went outside to see if a car had parked nearby with its radio playing. The music was not coming from any source that we could locate.

And then, I suppose, we began to move to the one place that we had all, on one level of awareness, been avoiding out of our wishful thinking. We began to move toward the altar that we had prepared to commemorate Rick's passing.

Melba began to weep as the entire family, including the children, heard the ethereal music coming from the ornaments around Rick's photograph. We all knew how much Rick loved music, especially Christmas music.

Strangely enough, after they had finally located the source of the beautiful, heavenly sounds, the music stopped.

But Louise suddenly had a clearer picture of what was occurring on that remarkable Christmas Eve. "The radio!" she shouted. "I wanted the radio off. Rick wants the radio on!"

Charles clicked on the old console model that they still kept in the living room. The very first sounds that flowed from the radio were the words of that poignant holiday song that promises, "I'll be home for Christmas."

Louise concluded her dramatic and inspirational account of the return of her son's spirit on Christmas Eve:

We all stood there, tears flowing freely, unchecked. We all hugged each other, and those of us who knew the words sang along with the radio. Charlie kept saying over and over, "I told you that Rick would find a way to let us know that he was all right. He did it. Rick came home for Christmas."

Our beloved son Rick had brought his family the greatest Christmas gift possible. He demonstrated the truth of the Savior's Christmas promise for all of his family. He gave his little children a proof of life eternal that will strengthen them all the days of their lives.

Contacting the Other Side with Instrumental Transcommunication

It is not surprising that Rick Horton communicated with his family through the radio. Utilizing earthly electronic devices for spiritual communication is not that uncommon. Such contact from the Other Side is known as instrumental transcommunication (ITC), and since the 1950s, there have been many reports of spirit messages manifesting on tape recorders, television sets, and, more recently, computers and fax machines.

Two respected researchers in the field of ITC, Jules and Maggy Harsch-Fischbach of Luxembourg, said that many of the first messages that they received from spirits of the dead were left on their telephone answering machine. One of those ethereal messages was left by Dr. Swejen Salter, who identified herself as a deceased scientist. The spirit of Dr. Salter described the afterlife as a paradise where the dead can literally create their own concept of Heaven, from an elegant mansion to a lush forest glen.

Parapsychologist Walter Uphoff, director of the New Frontiers Center in Oregon, Wisconsin, and one of the pioneer U.S. researchers in electronic communication with spirits of the dead, has stated his opinion that there is no death, only a change of worlds. Such electronic communications, he believes, offer strong evidence for the existence of an afterlife. He also commented that messages have been received from such "Timestream communicators" as Thomas Edison, Albert Einstein, Madame Curie, Jules Verne, and Michael Landon. Edison, it is quite well known, experimented with electronic communication with the spirit world before his own death in 1931.

The Image of Their Deceased Son Appeared on a Television Screen

In October 1995, four years after the death of their eighteen-year-old son Shaun in a tragic automobile crash, Sue and Trevor Paterson of Castleford, England, were stunned by the appearance of Shaun's face in photographs of their television screen.

The circumstances that led to such personal proof of survival for the Patersons began when Sue mentioned to a friend that she often felt a strange kind of coolness pass over her face and legs when she would sit watching television. The friend suggested that the next time Sue experienced such a chill, Trevor should take a picture of her. Later, when Sue again complained of the icy draft and Trevor snapped the photos, the processed film clearly showed a face that looked like Shaun's on the television screen—which had been switched off before the pictures were taken.

Maurice Grosse, an accomplished paranormal investigator with Great Britain's Society for Psychical Research, commented that he had visited the Patersons and examined the photographs in detail. In his opinion, the pictures had been taken with a normal camera with normal film and processed in a commercial store in the usual manner, and could not have been faked.

Reading the Palm of a Benevolent Being from the Other Side

In *Guardian Angels and Spirit Guides*, I tell of a situation similar to that of the Patersons, when the once-a-year manifestation of a ghostly hand in a Minnesota home was accidentally captured on film as it hovered just in front of the unplugged television set. Once I had obtained a copy of the photograph and saw that the lines in the palm of the mysterious hand were quite well formed and clear, I sent a life-size enlargement of the ghostly palm to Marge Tellez, an accomplished palmist in Sacramento, California.

Although Marge sent me a dozen or so pages of

analysis, which are discussed in greater length in the aforementioned book, the essence of her evaluation indicated a being possessed of an alert, logical mind, who could exert great powers of creativity; a being who was strong willed, loving, compassionate; who had established a balance between the physical and the spiritual; a being who lived a celibate, perhaps asexual existence.

And as I theorized in *Guardian Angels and Spirit Guides*, it would seem to me that these qualities are exactly those attributes that I would expect an angel or a benevolent spirit being to possess.

Seventy Percent of Widows Report Spirit Visitations from Their Husbands

Dr. Melvin Morse, author of *Transformed by the Light* and a professor at the University of Washington, has stated that his investigation of hundreds of post-death visits indicated that an astonishing 70 percent of widows reported spiritual visitations from their deceased husbands. Dr. Morse stressed firmly that these women were not crazy and they were not hallucinating. They experienced such visits as a part of real life.

"The visits occur while the women are awake, and they have real conversations with their deceased partners," Dr. Morse said during an interview with journalist Esmond Choueke in 1993. "Even when visits begin at night, widows who are sleeping are jolted awake, usually by a bright white, pulsating light.

Their first reaction is shock, then a peace and comfort washes over them. They are able to settle unfinished business or come to an acceptance that their husbands are okay. The husbands want to help the widows move on in life."

Dr. Morse also found that about 30 percent of widowers received visits from the spirits of their deceased wives and that more than half of the children who die return to appear before their parents.

From the correspondence that I have received from those who have returned the Steiger questionnaire of paranormal and mystical experiences—and from testimonies presented to me when I have spoken at such groups as Parents Without Partners—I can wholeheartedly agree with the findings of Dr. Melvin Morse that the spirits of deceased spouses still care for the partners they left behind. I very much suspect, however, that there are truly as many widowers as widows who have received visits from their beloved spouses on the Other Side. In my research, I have consistently found women much more open in discussing spiritual matters in general—and even more open in acknowledging their personal encounters with the paranormal.

Although the spiritual climate of our culture is in the process of changing toward a greater willingness to admit individual mystical experiences, many men, especially those over sixty, still have a need to appear at all times rational, logical, and emotionally independent. When a widow confides to close friends or relatives that her deceased husband visited her, she would be assured that whether or not she was believed, she would at least receive words of comfort and sympathy. A widower who is considering sharing a similar confidence would fear that such a revelation would only produce accusations of emotional weakness and mental imbalance. I have been elated over the years that so many men have felt confident to share the true extent of their personal spiritual encounters with me through the questionnaire. We have seen the percentages grow from approximately 27 percent male respondents in 1967 to nearly 50 percent in 1999.

A Very Special Anniversary Kiss

Edna and Phil Roberts were approaching their silver wedding anniversary. Phil promised Edna that the first gift she would receive from him would be a very special kiss for putting up with him for twenty-five years. Once he had proclaimed his intention of delivering that magnificent kiss, he ran down a list of extravagant gifts that he would add to her anniversary booty. He varied the list of presents so often that the only thing Edna was really certain of receiving for her silver anniversary present from Phil was that promised truly remarkable kiss.

Just a month before their anniversary, Edna received a call from a furniture store that unceremoniously presented her with the shocking information that her husband had just dropped dead of a heart attack while purchasing some new furniture for her. The day of the anniversary celebration turned out to be a day of mourning. Edna's and Phil's children and many friends and relatives came to visit her and console her, but when they had all left that evening, she was alone with an empty house and the gift of a new wristwatch that she had purchased for her husband.

Slowly she prepared for bed, dawdling over her cold cream session and watching an old movie on television in bed before she finally turned out her bedside lamp. "I had not lain there alone in the dark for very long when I was startled to see what appeared to be a pinkish-colored disk coming toward me," Edna said. "The disk continued to grow in size as it moved nearer to my bedside. Then, when it was just a few feet away, the disk transformed itself into the head and shoulders of my deceased husband, Phil." Edna continued her touching account.

His features hovered about four inches away from my face. His head kind of wavered, like it was trying to come into better focus, then it was very still and seemed very solid. There was a kind of illumination coming from Phil's face, and I could look deeply into his eyes. Then he kissed me, a lingering special kiss. I began to cry, but he gave me a wink and that whimsical smile that I knew so well. Then, as suddenly as Phil had appeared, he began to fade from my sight. He became smaller and smaller . . . until there was nothing but that little pinkish-colored disk . . . and then there was nothing. But my husband had kept his promise. I had received my special anniversary kiss.

Although there will always be the skeptics who will explain away the spirit visitation reported by Edna Roberts as an externalization of her loneliness and sorrow, the widow will always cherish that special anniversary kiss from her deceased husband as her personal proof that life continues beyond the grave.

Her Birthday Cakes Were Sent by a Ghost

Tosha Wiesen told me that on her husband, Herb's, last birthday before he passed away at the age of fifty-seven, he had received two elaborately decorated cakes, one from the family, another from an organization in which the Wiesens were active.

"Herb was like a big kid about birthdays," Tosha said. "And he was just as nuts about all the other holidays. He was so disappointed when our kids decided they were too old to go trick or treating on Halloween. I was afraid he was going to put on a costume and go out anyway. And for him to get two birthday cakes was like someone else winning the lottery. He just loved the special feeling that two birthday cakes gave him."

Tosha's birthday was the day after Christmas, and because she had come from a large family that had subsisted on a meager income, she had become accustomed to having her natal anniversary passed over without special notice. Of course the situation had been remedied years ago after their marriage, but she could not resist teasing Herb about his receiving two extravagantly large birthday cakes when she had gone for so many years without having received any cakes at all.

Herb took her in his arms and kissed her forehead. "Poor, poor little Tosha, no cake for her birthday all those many, many years. Well, my dear, this year I'll see to it that you receive two big cakes for your birthday!"

One week later, on August seventeenth, Herb died from a sudden heart attack. In her grief, the last thing on Tosha's mind was any thought of the birthday promise Herb had made her. But she was in for a surprise.

"A month after Herb's death, I sold the house," she said. "I couldn't bear living alone in the home in which we had shared so many years and so many dreams. I moved to an apartment in a much larger city in Michigan, just wanting to be by myself for a while and decide what would be the course of the rest of my life."

But October and November passed, December was almost gone, and it was the day after Christmas, her birthday, and she was all alone, feeling very depressed. "None of my family was near, and none of the few acquaintances I had made in the new city knew the date of my birthday," Tosha said, vividly recalling the terrible loneliness that she felt. "Herb had been gone since August, and I was lonely, depressed, and about to spend a night in solitude and misery."

But on that cold and icy night, Ginger Symons, a new acquaintance whom Tosha had met only weeks before at the church she had begun attending, traveled across the city by bus to deliver a cake and a carton of ice cream to her so that they might celebrate her birthday.

"But how did you know it was my birthday?" Tosha had to know.

Ginger explained that she had been walking home from work when a man with a big smile approached her. "I don't know his name," she shrugged, "but I'm certain that I've seen him at church. Anyway, he told me that it was your birthday and that you would be lonely without anyone there to celebrate with you. And he told me to be certain to get you a cake!"

Tosha knew that she had met no man at church to whom she had disclosed her birthdate. She was asking Ginger to do her best to describe the stranger when there came another knock at her door.

She answered the door to find Shelly Duncan, a young woman who lived in the apartment across the hall, standing there with a large cake box in her hands. "Happy birthday, Tosha," she said, stepping inside with the cake.

"But how did *you* know . . . ?"

Shelly smiled as she set the cheerily decorated birthday cake next to the extravagantly decorated cake that Ginger had brought. "Some guy who says he lives in the building—I'm certain that I must have seen him before—said that he had heard that it was your birthday and that you would be celebrating it all alone," she explained "He told me that I should be certain to get you a nice cake, but"—she laughed—"I see that you already have one."

Yes, she had two beautiful birthday cakes, just as Herb had promised her that she would. Tosha asked Shelly to tell her more about the man who had informed her of the birthday celebration.

"Kinda tall, heavyset, maybe," she began. "You know, the thing I really noticed about him was how his whole face seemed to light up when he told me about your birthday. He was like a big kid. I asked him if he was coming to your birthday, and he said he would be there in spirit."

"That's funny," Ginger said. "That's exactly what the man I spoke to said when I asked him to come along to the party, that he would be there in spirit."

Tosha's husband had kept his word from beyond the grave. He had seen to it that she received two special cakes for her birthday.

A Jealous Ghost Got His Revenge

According to Barbara Hovey of California, the spirit of her deceased husband appeared to her so that he might enjoy a last laugh at her expense. Walter Jurasko had been much older than she when they married. In fact, at fifty, he was two years older than her father.

Walter was a real jealous sort of man. I was only twenty-four, and I don't really think I knew what I was doing. It wasn't long before I was really feeling smothered by him. He wouldn't even let me go shopping by myself or have lunch with any of my girlfriends. Any socializing that I did do with my friends or family, Walter insisted take place in our home. Since he was an accountant who worked out of an office in our home, he was always there to keep an eye on me. I was probably too flighty for marriage, anyway, so it wasn't long before I charged mental cruelty, and irreconcilable differences, and filed for divorce.

Barbara Hovey admitted that once her divorce was final, she began to date again with a vengeance to make up for the seventeen months that she felt Walter Jurasko had stolen from her. Although in retrospect she admits that she should have known better, she fell in love with Barry Salzman, a handsome and very well-off young attorney. Before the end of the year, she had married him.

This time I was the jealous one. Barry said that he was rich enough so he didn't want me working, so I sat alone and bored at home until he returned from work. And sometimes that wasn't until one or two in the morning. "Working late at the office" became his mantra. But I had seen how attractive his secretary and one of his law partners were. I was continually stressed, worrying over how much time was spent in work and how much in hanky-panky.

Barbara had not heard any news of Walter Jurasko for over a year when, one night, as she and Barry were in their upstairs bedroom, the image of her first husband appeared at the foot of their bed.

He just stood there looking down at us. I didn't think of anything supernatural, I just kept thinking about how jealous I had made Walter and how I had hurt him. He appeared so real and so solid that I was fearful that he had somehow broken into our house to do Barry and me harm. But he just stood there looking at us—and then he started to laugh. He didn't say a single word, but he just stood there laughing for several seconds—then he turned and ran down the stairs.

At first when the image of Walter appeared, Barry was totally stunned. It was like he was paralyzed. Then when Walter turned and ran from the room, he grabbed the baseball bat he kept under his side of the bed and ran down the stairs in pursuit of a man he thought was some kind of sick pervert who had broken into our house.

After several minutes of searching the house and finding all the doors and windows securely locked tight, Barry returned, pale-faced, to their bedroom. "What in hell was that?" he demanded. "I know I saw a strange man in our bedroom. I know you saw him. But there is no sign of that weird guy anywhere in the house and no sign of any break-in. I know we don't do drugs, and I know that I didn't have too much to drink tonight—so what in hell did we see?"

Barbara decided against telling Barry that they had somehow encountered the image of her first husband.

If Barry had found no evidence of a break-in, then it was obvious that Walter had not *really* been there at all. What they had seen must have been some kind of really bizarre hallucination—a weird mutual one, because Barry described Walter in great detail.

Sleep was next to impossible for the remainder of the night, but that next morning at breakfast, Barbara found at least a partial answer to the mystery in the daily newspaper.

> I don't usually check the obituaries, but there it was right before my eyes. Walter had died of a sudden heart attack the day before. What we had seen in our bedroom had to have been his ghost. I had never really believed in such things, but both Barry and I had seen the image so solidly that he had even got out of bed to chase it with his baseball bat.
>
> I was still left with the mystery of why Walter was laughing at us—or, perhaps more specifically, at me. Such a jolly apparition surely didn't fit the stereotyped version of a mournful figure in a flowing white robe.

Barbara said that she didn't have long to wait for an answer to her enigma. Just a few days after the spirit of Walter Jurasko had appeared in their bedroom, Barry told her that their marriage had been a mistake. He knew now how much he really loved his law partner, and he told Barbara that he was filing for a divorce.

It was now very apparent to me why Walter's spirit had materialized in our bedroom. He was getting a good last laugh at me. He had been terribly jealous of me, just as jealous as I was toward Barry; and I had left Walter as coolly and abruptly as Barry was preparing to leave me. There I was—married and divorced twice in less than three years!

A few years later, Barbara married Jim Hovey, this time, it appears, successfully. "Walter's spirit never again manifested," she said. "I think that he was satisfied to have had that last laugh at me because he knew the pain that was about to come to me when I learned of Barry's infidelity. I think he decided to leave me alone once I had suffered at least one terrible heartbreak, just as he had."

Strange Things Happened in this Native American Center

In the cases that we have presented thus far in this chapter, the individuals who shared accounts of their contact with spirits of the dead have been able to recognize the entity involved in their ethereal encounters. Such is not always the case, for example, when an office building is haunted. The following fascinating story was presented to Jeff Rense and me for discussion on his popular international radio show, "Sightings."

I am a Native American woman who lived and worked in a large California city as a case manager and administrative assistant for a Native American assistance center. When the Federal Relocation program began in the 1950s, people from many different tribes began to pour into major cities around the nation from various reservations. Once in the cities, the federal government was to supply them with job training or jobs and a place to stay until they could get along on their own. Native American centers sprang up in urban areas to assist tribespeople with the difficult business of transition. Many of these relocated people were lonely in the cities. They missed their homes, their families and friends, and they felt like strangers in a strange new world. At the centers, they could spend time with other native people, share meals, enjoy powwows and social gatherings and take part in arts and crafts projects.

The phenomena that I witnessed occurred in a two-story building that had a large kitchen downstairs, a huge theater and dance hall upstairs, a full bar in the back, and several storefront offices at street level. Just before we moved into the building, one of the realtors told us that a strange thing had happened to him late one night when he had been alone painting one of the downstairs offices. He said he heard a lot of loud stomping, dancing, and drums coming from the dance hall above his head. He rushed upstairs to see who was there, but when he got there, it was dark and empty. It frightened him so much that he left and never worked in the building after dark again.

Four of us administrators were to live in the building, and the first night we slept on the floor in sleeping bags in the back office of the main hall. Around 3:00 A.M. we were awakened by tinkling bells and a swishing noise that sounded like a woman in a long skirt with a lot of material walking around. The tinkling sound went on night after night.

One evening several of us were sitting in chairs in the main hall. It was late, and we were just drinking coffee and talking when we heard a very loud crash in the next room. When we investigated, we were surprised to find nothing out of place.

One night as I was trying to sleep, I was disturbed for hours by the sound of the others moving heavy furniture around in the office above me. I could not imagine why they would be working so late and why they had decided to completely rearrange the office. Several times, just as I was about to drift back to sleep, it sounded as though they dropped a heavy desk right above me. I was extremely annoyed, and the next morning I bounded up the stairs to see what all they had done. Not a single piece of furniture had been moved. Everything was as it had been the day before.

On one occasion I was so frightened I couldn't move as I listened for hours to doors opening and closing, something heavy being dragged down the long, carpeted corridor, and the sound of those strange, tinkling bells. In addition to all the noises, the lights kept turning off and on.

One of the most persistent of the phenomena was

the occurrence of weird odors that would fill the rooms. Once we thought someone was making toast. The entire center smelled like toast. We checked for electrical problems and found none. On other occasions, the odor smelled like decaying flesh.

On one particular Saturday afternoon the center was closed, but some of us were watching a football game in the reception area of one of the downstairs offices. All of a sudden, we could hear my computer printing in my office at the back of the building. We looked at each other in shock. We were alone in the center, and my office door was locked so no one could have entered. When we went back to investigate, we found the printer *disconnected* from the computer, but it had printed out several pages. When we read what was printed, we saw that most of it was unintelligible, but then there were these words: *I have . . . I want . . . I love.*

One evening a few nights later, as the married couple were sleeping, the man awakened to see the figure of a woman standing over his wife. A woman in a white dress was seen by several people, including myself.

As older members of the community began to come around, we heard many stories about eerie happenings that had occurred in our center. People had been experiencing strange things there for years. I don't know who owns the building now, and I don't have the faintest idea who the entities were. But I can confirm that my claims are not unfounded.

As the administrators of the Native American center learned, restless spirits can become very noisy and make a lot of racket. In the next chapter, the entities from Shadow World that we shall encounter will provide us with some of the noisiest, most rambunctious, and most frightening demonstrations of other-worldly manifestations. They are the poltergeists.

CHAPTER THREE

Poltergeists—Entities from the Secret Places of the Spirit

In the serious tone of voice that he reserved for such occasions, David Webster had just finished asking the blessing over his family's dinner when two miniature glass ballerinas exploded on a dining room shelf just above his left shoulder.

His twelve-year-old daughter Krystina screamed and leaped to her feet, nearly upsetting the dinner table. "My ballerinas, what's happened to them?"

She ran from the table to survey the damage on the shelf on which she displayed her prized collection of beloved miniature dancing figures.

Webster pushed his chair back from the table and brushed glass fragments off his sleeve and shoulder. He, too, was puzzled by the mysterious shatterings of the tiny ballerinas. His wife, Sandra, had already gone after a broom and a dust pan, and his nine-year-old son Peter surveyed the scene with widened eyes. Two-year-old Miriam in her high chair had begun to cry, startled by the sudden explosions.

Krystina picked up one of the larger pieces, tears welling in her eyes. "Oh, no, it's Ingrid and Helga, two of my oldest ballerinas. And they've been broken into a dozen pieces!"

She had been collecting the miniatures since she was four years old, and there were now at least twenty of the dainty dancing girls frozen in various poses on shelves around the dining room, complementing her mother's collection of commemorative plates. "Daddy," she asked, "what could have made them explode like that?"

"I have no idea," Webster began, then, realizing that he was the authority figure who was supposed to have all the answers, he guessed, "Perhaps moisture, sudden condensation or expansion. Sometimes things like that happen to glass windows and doors."

Within a few minutes, the mess had been cleaned up. Sandra had replaced the broom and pan and comforted Miriam, and Krystina had rearranged her eighteen or so remaining glass ballerinas according to their age and favored status.

"Perhaps now we may resume our evening meal," Webster said, attempting to keep the exasperation from his voice. The roast beef had cooled perceptibly, and the gravy was well on its way to forming a greasy film on the surface of the serving bowl. "Krystina, dear, please stop sniffling like that."

"But, Daddy," she reminded him, "I've had Ingrid and Helga since I was four. They were my first ballerinas. Aunt Margaret gave them to me."

"Sweetie," her mother said, trying to soothe her daughter's injured feelings, "maybe we can find two ballerinas to replace them."

Krystina tried unsuccessfully to hold back the tears. "But they won't be Ingrid and Helga."

Webster was losing his patience. He had endured a long, hard day at the office. He was tired and hungry. "Krystina, stop that crying over two silly glass figures! You're too old to bother with such silliness, and we've spent far too much money on those ridiculous things as it is. Your mother tells me that you may need braces on your teeth, you want to take piano lessons, you want a new dress for some friend's party. Will your childish demands never end? Do you think I'm made of money? Just forget about replacing those glass ballerinas. Learn to place your values on more important—"

There may have been more to David Webster's lecture, but his rant was interrupted by the wall barometer spinning crazily away from the wall and smashing to the floor.

Then, before any of the family could move away from the table, each of Krystina's eighteen glass ballerinas exploded one by one, as if some invisible marksman had chosen the Webster living room for a shooting gallery.

Pictures were ripped off the walls by unseen hands.

A heavy stuffed chair upended itself, and books were scattered from their shelves.

The large bowl of gravy levitated above Peter's head and emptied its contents on his hair.

The climax of that evening's demonstration came when little Miriam was lifted from her high chair and set down in the bowl of mashed potatoes in the middle of the table.

The disturbance at the dinner table that evening was only the beginning of a two-week nightmare of demonic insanity that infected the Webster household. Cushions were removed from sofas; bedclothes were tossed about the rooms; screw-top bottles popped open and spewed their contents around the kitchen, bathroom, and basement.

The Websters suffered the frightening onslaught in silence. David Webster was a big, stern, church-going, no-nonsense type of fellow, and he would have been humiliated beyond that which he could bear if news of his family's private torment had leaked out to the press. Instead, the strict father imposed an exile on his family; and with the exception of a few close relatives and friends, the Websters rode out the devilish storm in complete isolation. David Webster may never have heard of a poltergeist before those two nightmarish weeks in August 1962, but without a doubt, he had played the unwilling host to one of these rambunctious and house-trashing entities.

Poltergeists and Puberty

Poltergeist is German for throwing or pelting ghost, but the majority of contemporary psychical researchers have come to agree that the invisible housebreaker is a berserk bundle of uncontrolled psychokinetic energy (that is, the direct action of mind on matter) rather than a rude and nasty spirit entity. Most investigators have also reached a consensus in attributing the disturbances to the presence of youngsters (especially females) entering puberty and beginning to define their sexual roles. Such psychokinetic displays as the levitation of crockery and furniture and the materialization of voices and ghostly images have also been reported among newlyweds during their period of marital adjustment.

The psychoanalyst Dr. Nador Fodor believed that the human body is capable of releasing energy in an unconscious and uncontrolled manner, thereby providing the psychic power for the poltergeist's pranks. Author-researcher Sacheverell Sitwell agreed that the psychic energy for such disturbances usually derives from the psyche of someone undergoing sexual trauma. In *Poltergeists* (University Books, New York, 1959) Sitwell conjectured, "The particular direction of this power is always toward the secret or concealed weaknesses of the spirit . . . the obscene or erotic recesses of the soul."

When Krystina gave me her account of the experience, she was in her mid-thirties and she, in retrospect, had begun to suspect that she may somehow have been the unconscious cause of the disturbances. Quite likely, she was correct in her mature suspicions of her pubescent resentment of her father's strict religious views and his cool, unsympathetic, almost indifferent, attitude toward child-rearing.

Diary of a Poltergeist

Here are excerpts from a diary kept by Lydia Kurtz during the two weeks she and her husband, Loren, were caring for their twelve-year-old grandson Martin while their daughter Heidi and her husband, Joe, were hospitalized after a severe automobile accident.

"Neither of us ever caught Marty throwing anything or breaking anything, but I strongly suspected him of being the center of the poltergeist manifestations we experienced during the time he stayed with us," Lydia wrote in her report to me. "I know that he somehow considered himself to blame for his parents' accident since the terrible crash occurred as they were coming to pick him up after hockey practice. I also know that he hated playing hockey and would rather be taking the piano lessons that he was forced to drop because of his father's athletic ambitions for him. What is more, I know that he was experiencing normal preadolescent sexual tensions, because two girls kept calling the house for him, and it was obvious that he didn't know how to handle female attention. I also found him very often looking through some of Loren's old *National Geographic* magazines, the ones with the bare-chested native girls."

Marty began his stay with the Kurtzes on a Tuesday night. For the first four days, things were as ordinary as one might expect a grandson's visit to be. Then on the fifth day, Saturday, Lydia began her "Diary of a Poltergeist":

Day One, Saturday: I found Marty crying on the couch. I asked him what was wrong, and he was evasive. I asked if he were concerned about his parents. He just got up and walked away. As he left the room, the ceiling globe above him shattered and pieces fell to the floor. Marty seemed not to notice and just kept walking away.

Day Two, Sunday: Marty went to church with us, but he sat through the service like a dummy, saying nothing, refusing to sing any hymns with us. I asked him to help me fix lunch. He was pouring water from a pitcher into a glass and it just seemed to explode. Marty seemed very frightened and begged me to understand that he didn't do it. I told him it was just some weird kind of accident.

Day Three, Monday: Marty literally ran in the door after school, as if something were chasing him. As he ran past two smoke detectors in the kitchen and dining room, each one of them went off.

Day Four, Tuesday: When Loren went in the living room to read his evening paper, all the lamps had been unplugged and their cords were tied into knots. Marty denied touching any of them.

Day Five, Wednesday: The old clock on Loren's desk seemed literally to fly to a corner of a bookcase eight or nine feet away, and although it crashed to the floor, it was not broken. Both Loren and I ob-

served this occurrence. Marty was upstairs study-
ing.

Day Six/Seven, Thursday/Friday: Sometime during the night, all thirty of my music boxes began to
play in the downstairs dining room. I keep my collection in a glass case, and the key is in my jewelry
box on my dresser.

Day Eight, Saturday: Even though Marty was
gone all day with his friends, the Thermos jug that
I had been filling for Loren to take with him fishing
exploded inside and shattered the glass lining.

Day Nine, Sunday: After church, I started the
washer and the dryer in the basement laundry
room, and as I began to walk back upstairs, they
both shut off. I found both cords pulled and twisted
into those strange knots.

Day Ten, Monday: When we got up in the morning, we found all the pictures in the living room,
dining room, and kitchen turned to the wall.

Day Eleven, Tuesday: Our son-in-law Joe was released from the hospital. Although it would be a
few more days before Heidi would be home, Joe
said he would take Marty off our hands. As we
hugged and kissed him good-bye, there was a loud
cracking noise in the ceiling above us.

Sexual Frustrations and Adjustments Can Attract Spirit Entities

A female medium of widely recognized paranormal
abilities once told me that she, a mature woman in her

late forties, was capable of manifesting more psychic phenomena when she was sexually frustrated.

"I can channel stronger spirit manifestations and make them last longer if I am sexually frustrated or if I have become sexually aroused," she said. "I find it more difficult to conduct an effective seance if I am satisfied sexually. Sometimes, during an especially good seance, however, I will reach orgasm as I am producing a materialization."

The medium said that she agreed only in part with those theories that maintain that the root cause of the poltergeist is primarily psychological. "I also believe that sexual frustration and longing of young people trying to adjust to sex or to marriage can attract many spirit entities in many different forms."

As my explorations of the Shadow World broadened and deepened, I came to agree with the medium that discarnate entities quite separate from the adolescent psyche, quite distinct from the sexual tensions of marital adjustment, can be attracted from other dimensions by the release of such primal human energy. I have also come to suspect that those who are experimenting with the regenerative life force and learning to adapt to their sexual desires and needs may transmit all sorts of powerful vibrations that may in some way activate old memory patterns that have permeated haunted rooms and places. In addition to reactivating long-dormant emotions of hate, sorrow, or fear impressed into the environment, these sensual shock waves might well attract the activities of certain shadowy entities best left undisturbed.

These Boots Were Made for Haunting

Lynda Peagler sent me a report of the manifestations that occurred in the small bungalow she and her husband, Gary, rented shortly after their marriage. It seems likely that their early period of marital adjustment created the psychokinetic energy that activated the spirit of a young wife who had been murdered there. They had only lived in the house about a week when Lynda was disturbed by a strange thudding noise, "like someone striking an empty cardboard box with a closed fist." On other occasions, she heard what seemed to be the sound of someone running up and down the stairs with heavy boots on their feet.

She heard the noises many times over the next two weeks, and once the racket sounded not more than a few feet above her head. Lynda began to have fainting spells, and when she regained consciousness, she would feel weak and drained of strength.

She resisted telling Gary about the bizarre disturbances for fear of inviting his mockery. She had discovered that her husband was a very materialistic young man who would not listen sympathetically to tales of things that went bump in the night.

She had also discovered a pair of women's white boots in the crawl space that served as a storage area above their bedroom. They were worn at the heels, as if they had seen a lot of wear. She recognized them as the style that used to be called go-go boots. She firmly believed that it was these boots she heard running up and down the stairs.

Then one evening when the newlyweds were hosting another young couple of their acquaintance, Lynda heard Gary calling her and the other woman from the kitchen, where they had been preparing a snack.

"There's someone in the house," Gary said excitedly. "A weird-looking, tall blond woman."

Their guest substantiated his claim, and the two young couples set about searching the small home. They found no sign of any intruder.

When they returned to the living room and the tray of snacks and drinks that the ladies brought from the kitchen, Gary said that he and the other man had been discussing an incident that had happened at work that day when a tall, blond woman had pushed open the draperies and looked in at them. Her hair had seemed to be wet, and it stuck to her face. Both men had seen the woman clearly, and they had watched her white boots under the draperies as she turned and walked away.

Since her hard-nosed, materialistic husband had seen something strange for which he could not account, Lynda unburdened herself and told them of the noises that had plagued her during the day and of the fainting spells that accompanied the sounds. She also told them about the old pair of women's white boots that she had discovered.

Lynda Peagler concluded her report by stating:

> We lived in that house for just a few more weeks, then we gave up and moved. We talked to a number of old-timers in the neighborhood who claimed

that the place was haunted by the ghost of a woman who had been drowned by her husband. We were told that the place was always for rent or for sale. Many families had lived in the house, but none of them had stayed for more than a few weeks at a time.

Marital Discord May Have Invited a Noisy Ghost to Their Trailer Home

One of the listeners to our monthly ghost quest on Jeff Rense's "Sightings" said that the eerie events that occurred within the thin metal walls of his family's trailer home when he was a child had forever shaped his life.

Prior to our parents' divorce, the shower would turn itself on. Father always blamed it on my two brothers or me, but we knew each other to be innocent. After the divorce, Father no longer wanted to sleep in the bedroom that he had shared with our mother, so he began sleeping on the couch. One night while he was sleeping, there came a loud rapping at our front door. Angrily he went to answer it, but there was nobody in sight. About that same time, we would awaken at nights dripping sweat, and Father would discover the furnace had been turned up full blast. Since it wasn't winter, no one would have gone near the furnace.

Some nights I would see the door to my older brother's room open by itself. I would hear footsteps walk down the hall, enter the bathroom, flush the toilet, then walk into the room I shared with my younger brother. I would sit up in my bed, unable to sleep because I could feel a dark presence as the invisible spirit paced through our room. As a child, this experience intensified my fear of engulfing darkness.

One night as we sat watching television in the living room, the hall light began to flicker on and off. Father asked one of my brothers to turn it off. As soon as he would turn it off, it would turn itself back on. My brother turned it off once more before he came back into the living room. Just as he sat down, the light came on again and violently flickered off and on, as if in spite.

We didn't want to move, so Father thought he would bring a preacher into the trailer and pray the spirit away from our home. A local preacher, Bible in hand, went into the middle bedroom where we all felt the spirit most often. While my brothers and I stayed in the kitchen to watch over a pot of pasta for the night's supper, we saw the dark shadow of a child form between the kitchen and the hallway. Father said that when the preacher walked into the bedroom with the Bible and began to pray, the entire room filled up with some kind of fog. The preacher thought the spirit left when the fog drifted out of the room.

Later that night, we found out that it wasn't so easy to get the spirit to leave. There was such a pounding on the outside of the trailer that we ran outside to see whatever could be the source of the racket. Whatever it was, it could not be seen, and the pounding just kept hammering away, circling and circling the trailer until it finally quieted down.

After spending over a year with this restless soul, we finally moved out. Later, we found out from a friend that the trailer burned down after we left. Almost twelve years later, we drove through the trailer park and discovered that our old lot was still vacant. No one had ever wanted to set their trailer down on that spot.

A Police Officer's Account of a Poltergeistic Onslaught

Police Sgt. Daniel Goldsmith told of an encounter that he and three fellow officers had with poltergeistic manifestations in an apartment in a midwestern city.

"We had no idea what to expect when we got the call around eleven o'clock that night," Sgt. Goldsmith began. "My partner Les Henges and I were told that a lady had complained that someone was banging on her walls, so we didn't know if we were going to have to quiet some noisy party animals in the next apartment or some cranky neighbor who might have thought the woman was making too much noise in her apartment."

When officers Goldsmith and Henges arrived at the address that had been dispatched to them, they quickly discovered that the complaint had been filed by a woman who lived on the third floor. "That meant no one could be making noise above her, because she was on the top floor," he said.

As the men walked down the hallway toward her apartment, they could hear nothing that could qualify as raucous party sounds. Maybe they had lucked out, and the complaint of a disturbance had taken care of itself.

But the minute the two officers stepped inside the apartment of Dolores Compeau and her eleven-year-old daughter Sophie, they could hear the terrible pounding sounds that seemed to be issuing from all around them.

As Sgt. Goldsmith stated in his report of the incident:

> Mrs. Compeau appeared on the brink of nervous collapse, and her daughter was curled into a semi-fetal position on the couch. It was incredible. You stepped back out into the hall, and you couldn't hear a thing out of the ordinary. Yet the second you moved back into the apartment, you could hear what sounded like someone pounding the walls with a hammer. I told Les to check up on the roof while I tried to calm Mrs. Compeau and her daughter.
>
> According to Mrs. Compeau, the disturbance had begun as they were finishing the evening meal, about six o'clock. They were discussing some problem that Sophie was having in school when the pounding had begun. Not so loud at first, kind of like someone knocking on the wall with his knuckles. They knew that they had raised their voices to some degree, and they thought that they might have disturbed the elderly man who lived in the next apartment. When the pounding got louder, Mrs. Compeau called her neighbor to see why he was so upset with them, and he said that he had no idea what she was talking about. It surely was not he pounding on the wall.

I felt along the walls, but it was the strangest thing. The pounding didn't really seem to be coming from the walls at all. I couldn't really tell where the sounds were originating. Les came back down from checking the roof and said that he could find nothing up there that could possibly make such noises. I told him to call officers Bulinski and Lindsay to come and help us go through the apartment house. I thought right away that maybe someone had rigged some kind of electronic device in Mrs. Compeau's apartment as some kind of cruel prank. Such proved not to be the case.

When officers Bulinski and Lindsay entered the Compeau apartment, the phenomena dramatically increased their scope and intensity. As all four police officers watched, the dinner plates, which were still on the kitchen table, lifted themselves into the air and smashed against the wall. As Officer Bulinski rushed forward to examine the unexpected and unexplained mess, a kitchen chair scooted across the room, slamming into his knees and nearly tripping him.

"And all this time," Sgt. Goldsmith said, "the infernal pounding kept right on, not missing a beat. When the plates and the chair started to move, Sophie began to scream hysterically that she wanted to leave the apartment. At the same time, Officer Lindsay covered his ears with his palms and said that he had to get out of the room. There was some kind of weird vibration in the place that was making his eardrums feel that they were about to explode."

Sgt. Goldsmith could clearly see that Lindsay was in

extreme distress. His face was ashen, and he appeared about to faint. "I ordered him to go down to the basement and check the heating to determine if there might be anything there to account for the strange disturbances. When he hesitated, I could tell that he was genuinely afraid to go alone, so I told Les to go with him. Lindsay was a big, tough guy, but he was scared of something in that apartment."

Officer Bulinski called Sgt. Goldsmith's attention to another kitchen chair slowly moving backward. As the two officers and Mrs. Compeau watched, the chair did a complete flip, then set down gently again in its former upright position.

Sgt. Goldsmith concluded his account.

I asked Mrs. Compeau if she had someplace that she could go for the night. She said that she had a cousin who lived across town. I suggested that she call the cousin and request a night's sanctuary, pack a few things in a bag, and I would have Officer Lindsay drive her and Sophie to wherever they needed to go. All this time, Sophie had been whimpering and crying, and, from time to time, emitting this hellish scream.

Once Mrs. Compeau and her daughter left the apartment, Officer Henges and Officer Bulinski and I stayed and puzzled over the continued sounds of the pounding and did our best to come up with some kind of rational explanation for what we had experienced that night. We remained for another fifty minutes or so. The pounding was becoming quieter and less frequent. Approximately every ten minutes, the entire apartment would seem to tremble, as if we were experiencing an earthquake. And then the disturbances stopped altogether.

It seems to me that we had observed genuine poltergeist phenomena that night. We checked everywhere in that apartment building for some kind of ordinary physical explanation for the things we observed and came up blank. From what I have read on the subject, a young person, especially a female, serves as the center for such disturbances, and I wonder if Mrs. Compeau and her daughter had been experiencing an emotional conflict of greater duration than an argument about school over dinner that night. Officer Henges stepped into a number of apartments around and below the Compeau apartment, and neither he nor any of the occupants could detect any unusual sounds—certainly not the terrible pounding that we had experienced in the Compeau apartment. Officer Lindsay pointed out that there was a large cemetery across the street, and he admitted that he thought that he had seen and felt spirit presences in the Compeau apartment. Later, I learned that Mrs. Compeau and her daughter had moved out, because Sophie refused to return to the apartment. I think they also moved out of the city soon afterward.

From Poltergeist Attacks to a Peaceful Resolution from the Other Side

Carol Gieschen knew that, because of religious reasons, her grandfather did not approve of Jack Sullivan's courting her. Grandpa Gieschen had strong convictions that one must marry within one's faith, and it seems quite likely that it was the psychological tension her grandfather created within her that led to a flurry of Poltergeist activity around the eighteen-year-old girl.

For a period of nearly two weeks, Jack's visits to the Gieschen home were accompanied by violent outbursts of psychokinetic energy. Mrs. Gieschen's favorite vase shattered as the two young people held hands on the sofa. Invisible hands banged on the piano keyboard, and the piano stool jumped across the living room floor and struck Carol smartly across the shins.

One night as the young lovers had just finished making a tray of cookies in the kitchen and were allowing them to cool, the entire two dozen chocolate chip cookies burst into flames.

As in most poltergeist attacks, the unconscious energy center of the disturbance received the brunt of its abuse and physical torment. Stigmatalike scratches were seen to appear on Carol's upper arms; and on one occasion, teeth marks appeared just below her shoulder blades.

To add to the tension, Grandfather Gieschen had moved in with the family about the time that Jack's courtship of his granddaughter had begun, so they never knew when he might emerge from his room to harass them.

"You're to blame for these disturbances," Grandpa Gieschen said one night, advancing on Jack with his cane. "To mix religions is to do the devil's work, and you've brought the devil upon us."

The old man swung his cane and caught Jack stoutly across his left shoulder. Jack jumped to his feet, dazed, angry, but restrained by his sweetheart.

"You old buzzard . . . if you were thirty years younger," Jack said, grimly clenching his fists.

In the kitchen, they could all hear the sounds of dishes shattering in the cupboards.

The poltergeist activity eventually spent its psychic energy, and the vortex of paranormal disturbances subsided. In spite of Grandpa Gieschen's incessant fulminations, neither Carol's nor Jack's parents were against a religiously mixed marriage, and they gave their blessings for the young people to be married.

Sadly, Grandpa Gieschen contracted pneumonia a month before the wedding date and passed away in an oxygen tent in the hospital. In spite of their annoying quarrels over religion and her choice of a husband, Carol was genuinely sorrowful when the old man died.

A few psychic strands of unconscious guilt over marrying outside her religion and against her grandfather's wishes may have contributed to the phenomena that visited Carol and Jack on their wedding night.

The newlyweds had checked into the nearest possible motel, eager to consummate their marriage. They had no sooner gone to bed, however, when they were sharply distracted from the marital rite by a loud knocking on the wall beside them. They tried desperately to ignore the sound, to blame it on an inconsiderate person next door—but the more the particular vibration of the knocking intruded on their lovemaking, the more they both realized that it sounded very much like Grandpa Gieschen's cane hitting the wall.

As they watched in amazement, a glowing orb of light appeared beside their bed. As the illumination grew and took shape, they were astonished to see a wispy outline of Carol's grandfather standing before them.

Then, as the features congealed and assumed a more definite shape, Carol somehow managed to form functional speech despite her fear and surprise. "He's . . . smiling. Grandpa's smiling!"

As the newlyweds lay in each other's arms, they saw the image of Grandpa Gieschen smile, move his cane aloft, then make the sign of the cross with it. He remained before them for just a few more seconds before he waved his hand in a gesture of farewell and disappeared.

"He blessed us, Jack," Carol said, tears welling in her eyes as she watched the last of her grandfather's ethereal form fading away. "He understands things better now that he's on the other side. Earthly differences in religion, skin color, politics, or anything else just don't matter over there."

CHAPTER FOUR

People Who Attract Ghosts

One of the questions that I am asked most frequently is whether or not a ghost can move with
a person or a family.

The answer is yes. And I suspect that most people
who ask me that question already know the answer,
for they have probably had the unique experience of
realizing that a ghostly entity packed up its ethereal
baggage and moved with them that time when they
were transferred from Ohio to Oregon.

What is more, the majority of individuals who have
experienced an other-worldly fellowship with no-
madic entities really don't seem to mind that the spirit
presences have followed them around the country.

Over the past forty years, I have received so many
reports from people who have moved across the country only to find that the same strange globe of blue
light that manifested in their bedroom in New Jersey is

hovering above them in New Mexico. Whether these mobile inhabitants of Shadow World manifest for their patron humans as angelic beings, ghostly figures, the aforementioned globe of blue light, or UFO phenomena, there seems little doubt in my mind that some people are what I term "spirit magnets." These men and women find themselves haunted for years on end no matter where they go. And sometimes they learn that it has run in the family—the same spirit entity that may have first attached itself to a grandparent or a great-grandparent has been inherited along with the furniture and the silverware.

I have found that those men and women who are spirit magnets have a deep spiritual energy that attracts certain entities that find their human warmth and kindness very comforting. And it is fortunate that the vast majority of spirit magnets attract benign entities who do them no ill.

It should come as no surprise that benevolent beings are attracted to the same kind of people that we humans admire most in our species. Spirit magnets are people with both passion and compassion, outgoing individuals who remain sensitive to the feelings and needs of others. They are basically optimistic people, slow to anger, at peace with themselves, and more concerned with spiritual, rather than materialistic, advancement.

Unfortunately, not all spirit magnets activate benign entities in every instance. In certain cases, a pre-existing haunting phenomenon of a negative or evil origin can seize upon the psychic sensitivity of a spirit magnet and utilize it for its own foul expression.

They Rented a House on the Edge of Hell

One of the strangest and most disturbing cases of a couple becoming a magnet for negative creatures from the Shadow World was told to me some years ago by George and Tina Martell. Their story began in 1974 when they and their friends Rick and Anna Delapena decided to cut down on their expenses by renting a house together.

"We had attended college together in Illinois and had been friends," Tina began in her account of their eerie experiences. "Rick and George had been on the same intramural softball team, and Anna and I had been in a number of classes together. We had double-dated a number of times, and we had both married shortly after graduation in June. We ran into each other a couple of months later when we happened to be job-hunting in the same medium-sized city in Wisconsin."

When the two couples compared notes over hamburgers and fries in a fast-food restaurant, they freely admitted that they were feeling a very tight economic squeeze.

George and Tina had been staying with relatives while they searched for an apartment, and Anna and Rick had been renting a room in a cheap motel until they could move into something better. And none of the jobs for which they had applied were commensurate with their college educations. Before they parted company that afternoon, they had come up with the plan of renting a house together to economize.

"We laughed about being hippies and starting our own commune, like the flower children did in the 60s, but we all thought it was a good idea," George said, continuing the narrative. "We had all noticed that there were some big old houses in the city that appeared to be sitting empty. Some of them appeared to be in pretty tough shape, but we figured they might rent fairly inexpensively, and we could spend a little time to fix one up to be comfortable enough to get us through our economic crunch."

After a period of house-hunting, they found a very large three-story house on the outskirts of the city that rented for a very low sum. It didn't take long for the two couples to move in, for neither of them had any furniture or many possessions. And strangely enough, the mansion had been rented to them fully furnished.

"Neither Rick nor George was terribly impressed with the antique furniture," Tina recalled, "but Anna and I were blown away by the elegance of the furnishings. The carpets, the paintings, the plush furniture— we felt like we were interlopers in some old millionaire's mansion, and we just laughed at the guys grumping around and turning up their noses at 'the old junk.'"

The fellows did take great notice of the full-length portrait of the blonde woman that hung above the majestic fireplace in the living room. She was a tall, regal woman in her mid- to late thirties, Tina and Anna guessed, dressed in an elegant purple gown with white lace at the throat. She had been painted leaning slightly against the very same fireplace above which her portrait hung, so there seemed little question that she had once been the lady of the house.

"A real babe," Rick had assessed the portrait approvingly.

But Anna had shuddered as she studied the delicate features. "Those blue eyes of hers just seem to look right back at you. Like she would know what you were thinking. And they seem to follow you around the room wherever you walk."

Rick nodded agreement. "They paint some pictures that way. My grandmother has a portrait of Jesus with eyes like that. They just seem to look at you wherever you move in the room."

"We could always take the picture down if it bothers you," George suggested.

But they all agreed that the portrait should remain where it was. Somehow, they felt they would be violating the essence of the old mansion if they removed the picture of its once elegant mistress from her commanding position above the fireplace.

"Rick and Anna, who had degrees in education, had managed to get jobs as substitute teachers, and since one of the regular teachers had just had a baby and another had been in a car accident, it looked as though they wouldn't have any trouble making their share of the rent," Tina said. "George had a job as a clothing store manager that would start in a few days, and I had decided to accept the position of teller at a small bank that would be available at the beginning of the next week.

"Anyway, George and I were home alone rearranging some of our things in the kitchen when we clearly heard the sound of someone running up the stairs. Thinking that either Anna or Rick had come home unexpectedly, we came out to the living room and called upstairs."

They received no answer, yet George and Tina could hear the unmistakable sounds of someone clomping nosily in the upstairs hallway and then, to their utter disbelief, coming back down the stairs and out the front door.

"When we told Anna and Rick that night over dinner, they laughed and thought we were joking," George said. "We couldn't blame them. If the situation had been reversed, we probably would have laughed at them. When we insisted that we were not making it all up, they quieted down, but Tina and I caught them smiling and winking at each other."

Anna stopped smiling and winking two nights later. Tina and George were awakened by screams and shouts coming from the Delapenas' bedroom.

When they rushed in to see what was happening, they were shocked to see Anna thrashing about on the bed, her hands grasping at something near her throat.

"She says something is trying to choke her!" Rick shouted in explanation of his wife's bizarre behavior.

"As we watched in amazement, Anna appeared to

be wrestling with some invisible assailant," Tina said. "Rick was ashen-faced. He moved closer to pry Anna's hands from her throat, and something appeared to kick him in the stomach and knock him backward over a chair. I know it wasn't Anna who kicked him, because her legs appeared to be held down by some invisible force. Only her arms were free, and her elbows moved wildly back and forth as her hands tried to lift something from her throat that was trying to kill her. Her eyes were bulging, and the veins on her hands and arms stood out as if under great strain."

While Tina helped Rick to his feet, George rushed forward to help Anna. He has said that he will never forget being punched in the face by an invisible fist. He stumbled back away from the bed, stunned, bleeding from his nose.

And then, suddenly, Anna was lifted from the bed and dropped to the floor with such force that her ankle twisted sickeningly beneath her and her head struck the corner of a dresser.

"Anna lay there dazed, gasping for breath," Tina said. "I knelt beside her and straightened the ankle that was swelling beneath her. 'He tried to kill me,' she said in a hoarse whisper. 'This ugly little dwarf tried to kill me.'"

The four young newlyweds were puzzled. Had Anna just had the ultimate nightmare? Was it she that somehow kicked and punched Rick and George as they tried to help her?

None of them wanted to speak aloud the thoughts that were churning over in their minds. And what about the mysterious footsteps George and Tina had heard two days ago?

With a painfully swollen ankle and bruises around her throat and face, Anna had to call in sick after only three days as a substitute teacher. She told the stressed and agitated principal that she was sorry, but she had had an accident. She would try to be back at work as soon as possible.

After Rick left for his teaching assignment, George and Tina took Anna to a medical clinic.

"The doctor, a stocky, fatherly man in his sixties, was concerned about Anna's condition, and it was obvious from his line of questioning that he suspected spousal abuse," Tina said. "I assured him that the man sitting looking at magazines in the waiting room was *my* husband and that her husband wasn't responsible for her injuries, either.

"When he asked where we lived, he got really quiet and peculiar. We heard him mumble something about Anna's injuries not being surprising considering the house we were living in, but when we asked him to explain, he would say no more."

When the two women pressured him to tell them what he had meant, he finally responded tersely and enigmatically. "I'm sorry. I spoke out of turn. Sometimes I fear I might be getting senile. A doddering old man. I've lived in this city off and on since I was a boy. Let us just say that the house in which you are living has a certain history, a somewhat unpleasant history."

"Define *unpleasant*, the two women insisted.

"Things happened there around the turn of the cen-

tury," he said softly, as if he didn't wish to be over-
heard. "Terrible things. Perhaps even murder. But to
speak of it now is silly. Superstitious nonsense. Next
I'll be telling you ghost stories."

And then the doctor turned and walked brusquely
from the room, muttering about all the patients who
were awaiting his care.

During the next two days, while Anna was recover-
ing from her injuries, the three of them heard the footsteps running up and down the stairway. "I've got to
be back at school soon," Anna said. "There's no way
I'm staying alone in this house when you two start
work."

"Whatever else lived in that house besides us, it also
slammed doors and turned the water faucets on and
off," George said. "One night, as we were eating dinner in the dining room, we all saw the huge sliding
doors that separated the rooms pushed open by an invisible hand—and we all felt a cold breeze blow past
us.

"When we locked the doors that night, Rick said
that we were really locking up to protect the outside
world from what was living with us on the inside."

And then, right after Rick had made his astute observation, he turned toward the stairway and said,
"Whatever is in this place, hey, take it from me, you
stink!"

He was rewarded for his insult by the manifestation
of an incredibly foul, nauseating odor that hung around
the stairway for days.

* * *

At the end of their first week in the house, the two couples held a council to decide whether or not they should move. The disturbances were annoying and occasionally frightening, but there had been no other physical assaults such as the one that had kept Anna from her job for two days. All four of them were working days, so they could band together in the evenings.

Besides, they reasoned, maybe they had all overreacted. The sound of footsteps running up and down the stairs could be boards creaking as the old mansion settled. And maybe Anna had had just a really bad nightmare about a murderous dwarf. Most of the other bizarre phenomena could be attributed to wind finding its way through cracks in the walls, or even rats scurrying around in the dark.

After all, they were modern men and women, college-educated, sophisticated, intelligent. George and Rick blamed their occasional spookiness on all the creepy old antique furniture in the mansion.

They would stay in the house, bear the random weirdness, and save their money.

The morning after their council had voted in favor of frugality, a new manifestation occurred that may have been designed to make them reconsider their decision.

As the two couples were having breakfast a few minutes after seven o'clock, they heard what at first they thought was someone in the driveway with a lawnmower but Rick, an antique car buff, recognized the sound as that of the motor of an old roadster from the 1920s.

As they sat silently for a few moments in puzzlement, they heard a murmur of two distinctively different male voices and one female voice.

When they crowded to a window facing the front drive, they could see nothing, but the phenomena, which progressed into what appeared to be a violent argument between the two men, culminated with the sound of gunshots and a woman's scream.

The sounds of the ghostly argument and apparent murder occurred on two consecutive mornings.

When the two couples still gave no sign of moving, yet another disturbance was added to the repertoire of the haunting.

As they were sitting down to their evening meal one night just after sunset, they were startled to hear a woman's scream from the top of the stairs. There were the noises of a brief scuffle, then the sound of a body tumbling down the stairs, stopping with a heavy thud against the base of the banister.

Later that same evening, as George was in the basement getting a jar of fruit, something knocked him off a box as he stood on tiptoe, reaching for the highest shelf.

"I experienced a brief sensation that something was rushing toward me from out of the shadows just before it slammed into my knees," George said. "I had an impression that something like a large dog or some kind of big animal had struck me. And then I could hear it breathing, panting, from a dark corner of the fruit cellar. I admit that I was afraid to move.

"I yelled for Rick and told him to bring a flashlight with him. When he joined me, he directed the beam toward the corner where we could both hear the thing panting. The light appeared to make whatever it was scurry toward another dark section of the old basement."

After they had lived there nearly three weeks, Anna's parents, Deidre and Fred Seevers, who lived in another community only a few hours' drive away, came late on Friday afternoon to visit for the weekend.

Anna had often told her friends about her mother's psychic abilities. For years she had made accurate predictions about events that would occur to members of her family. There had been times in her early adolescence when having a "witch" for a mother had been a source of embarrassment for Anna, but during the 60s it had been cool to have a mom who could read Tarot cards and work astrology charts for her friends.

Deidre, a tall woman in her late fifties, was barely inside the door of the mansion when she shivered slightly and said that there was evil within. Anna grimaced. "Just want we wanted to hear, Mom."

As the two couples helped the Seevers with their luggage, Deidre stopped in front of the portrait of the elegant blonde lady that hung above the fireplace and nodded knowingly. "She's still the mistress of the mansion."

Then Deidre smiled as her large brown eyes surveyed the living room. "There are lots of people who share this big old house with you."

Tina remembered how matter-of-factly Deidre made her pronouncements. "She was, like, oh, you've got lots of houseguests for the weekend. No big deal. But she made me shiver, and I felt that I could bump into an invisible person at any moment. I could tell that Deidre was just bursting to tell us more, but it was obvious that her husband was not especially enthusiastic about her gifts."

Deidre walked from room to room, picking up various impressions as she moved through the old mansion. Later that night, after dinner, Anna asked her mother to share whatever vibrations she had accumulated during her psychic evaluation of the house.

"She told us that the blonde lady in the portrait had been involved in a love triangle with her husband and her husband's business partner," Tina said. "Her husband had pretended to be away on a business trip and had shot his deceitful partner as he drove up to the mansion one morning to keep a lover's tryst with his wife. The partner had been severely wounded, but he had lived. The blonde lady's husband, knowing the police would soon arrive to arrest him, struggled with her and accidentally pushed her down the stairs. When he realized that he had killed her, he was stricken with remorse and hanged himself in the basement."

The two couples sat in complete silence as Deidre described other entities whose impressions she had received. "There's an elderly woman who seems to have been poisoned. And a young man who also fell to his death down the stairs. He had been running through the house, screaming, convinced there was some kind of monster after him. And there's a child in here, a little girl, who was smothered in her sleep by that same monster. They thought she had died of pneumonia, but it was some kind of evil creature."

Anna told her mother about the "ugly dwarf" that had tried to strangle her.

Deidre listened intently to her daughter's description of that awful night. When Anna finished her account, she added an important correction: "It's not a dwarf, though. It's more like . . . oh, what do you call those things?"

"A troll," Tina spoke up.

"Yes," Deidre agreed, "that's right. A troll . . . or some kind of demon."

Tina then admitted that she had encountered some grotesque being in the hall one night when she got up to use the bathroom. "It was hairy, covered with dark bristles. It was as big as Rick or George, but it was bent over, kind of like it was a humpback or something. It had long clawlike fingernails, and it was ugly, with a face like a twisted ape."

Fred Seevers stood up, telling everyone that there had been enough of such pleasant bedtime conversation, enough to guarantee nightmares for everyone. A very conventionally religious man, Fred then suggested that everyone join hands as he led the group in a prayer for God's protection and the guardianship of angels while they slept.

*   *   *

The power of prayer was evidently in full force that night, for the mansion was unusually quiet.

The next day also passed without any noticeable manifestations. It was almost as if the phenomena were staying out of Deidre's way. But the vibrations of the place were still accessible to her psychic radar, and she was steadily picking up impressions throughout the weekend.

When she was alone with Anna and Tina in the kitchen preparing dinner on Saturday night, she issued a somber warning. "I don't wish to upset you. I know that you are living here to save money, but I think you should move as soon as possible. There is something inhuman that lives in this house. I'm not talking about the spirits of those who have shed their mortal shells. Whatever this thing is, it was never human. And it is evil. I am not easily frightened, but whatever this creature is, it has me terrified."

The next afternoon, as Anna's parents were preparing to leave, that invisible monster grabbed Deidre and threw her to the floor in front of the fireplace. It was apparent that it was attempting to choke her, just as it had when it had seized Anna by the throat.

"We stood by helplessly," Tina said. "George and Rick tried to wrench Deidre free of the invisible force, but it brushed these two men, each of them nearly two hundred pounds, aside as if they were small children.

"Then Fred, who had been loading their luggage into their car, came rushing in and began calling on the name of God to banish the creature back to the darkness. He stood there demanding the invisible monster release his wife and he summoned all attending angels to drive the beast back to hell. Then he bent down and picked up his gasping, choking wife. We all felt a rush of cold air as the demon left its prey and departed the room."

Fred Seevers did not mince words. "You kids have moved into a hell house. It harbors nothing but evil. Take my advice and move out of here as quickly as you can."

Deidre, whose voice was now but a whisper, said that she had been "talking" telepathically to the elegant blonde lady in the portrait when the ugly troll-like creature had come at her from out of the shadows. Its talons had reached for her throat and she knew that it wanted to kill her.

"Leave this house of the demon spawn," she gasped, repeating her husband's advice. "Last night I saw in a dream that this place will soon burn down. Fire from Heaven will rain down upon this hellhole and burn it to the ground."

George and Tina told me that the two couples made their final decision to leave the terrible place a few nights later when something managed to crawl under the covers on Anna and Rick Delapena's bed and clamp its teeth onto Anna's foot.

"Anna said that it was a huge bat," Tina said. "I thought it looked like an owl. George said it was a crow, and Rick thought it was some kind of hawk. Whatever it was, it was big and black with a huge wingspan and a terrible beak that seemed determined to bite off Anna's foot."

It had taken the two men to beat and to pry the wretched winged creature off Anna's foot. Rick smashed it several times with his tennis racket, and the thing still managed to crash through a window in the hallway and make its escape.

"We started moving out the next day," George said. "We didn't care if we had to stay in a motel for a while until we found some decent apartments. We just wanted to get out of the cursed place."

About ten days after the Martells and the Delapenas moved out, the mansion was struck by lightning and burned to the ground. It had been as Deidre Seevers had foreseen: "fire from Heaven" had consumed the hellhole.

But that was not the end of the ordeal for the Delapenas, George and Tina explained as they continued their account.

The two couples each managed to obtain fairly nice apartments in different sections of the city. Although they were now separated and worked different jobs and hours, they still managed to get together every few weeks and go to a movie, a ball game, or eat dinner at a restaurant. They seldom spoke of their ordeal in the accursed mansion. It was as if they honored an unspoken agreement not to resurrect any of those frightening, unpleasant memories.

"About six months later, Anna called me one night, sobbing hysterically," Tina said. "She told me that the

thing had found her again and she had seen it standing in a corner of their apartment one night when Rick
was working late. It had just stood there and leered at
her. She hadn't said anything to her husband, but three
nights later when they came home, they found their
bedclothes slashed to ribbons, as if some wild beast
had torn at the covers and pillows. Deidre had come
over, gone into trance, and told her that the beast had
tracked her down. She had advised them to move as
quickly as possible."

George and Tina were extremely discomforted by
the telephone call. Just between them, they had wondered why it was that the most violent manifestations
seemed always to attack Anna. And when Deidre
Seevers had visited, the hostile vibrations seemed focused upon her.

Could it be possible, they had speculated, that some
people, perhaps even some families, could serve as
some kind of magnets for such phenomena?

"Rick and Anna moved out of that apartment and
managed to find another that was farther away from
their teaching jobs, but somehow it seemed safer, more
secure," Tina continued. "But after about four or five
months, the monster found them again. It was truly as
if it kept seeking Anna out, as if it had some kind of
vendetta going against her. That next summer, they
moved out of the city and took teaching positions in a
city in northern Michigan, hundreds of miles away."

The two couples kept in touch by letter and telephone, and things seemed to be going well for the Delapenas for about a year.

"Then, in late 1977, we heard that eerie phenomena had begun occurring in their bedroom and something heavy had sat on Rick's chest one night and scratched his face," Tina said. "After that incident, they had both suffered from terrible nightmares, and they decided to move again. This time they moved to a larger city in upstate New York, and it seemed that they finally outdistanced the monster. Anna told us that they had not seen the ugly thing since 1977."

George and Tina had remained in contact with Anna's parents, Deidre and Fred Seevers, who lived in a lovely lakeside home just a few hours' drive from them.

"Although we had moved to Milwaukee in 1976, the Seevers were still within easy driving distance of us, and we would drop in for coffee whenever we were in the vicinity," George said. "In 1978, just a few months after we had last heard from Anna concerning the nightmarish entity, the Seevers invited us to spend a weekend at their home. Since their place was as beautiful as a resort with a magnificent view of the lake and surrounding woods, we happily accepted. At that time we had Timmy, who was three, and Tina was pregnant with Lisa."

After a wonderful meal of venison, the two couples enjoyed a brandy in the living room with its awe-inspiring view of the moonlight playing on the surface of the lake. Tina had put Timmy down in the guest room, and the two couples were discussing the Camp David summit between Sadat and Begin that had been arranged by President Carter when the child suddenly began screaming in terror.

"When Deidre and I entered the room where Timmy slept, we were startled by something shuffling toward us from the shadowed corner of the room," Tina said.

"To our horror, the wretched troll-like monster was coming toward us and reaching out toward Timmy. In the moonlight that streamed in through the large picture windows, we could see that thick, dark hair covered its features except for its large, serpentine eyes and its gaping mouth with jagged teeth and protuberant fangs. Timmy was screaming for his mommy, and his mommy was screaming for Daddy!"

Fred and George reached the bedroom and were literally stunned when they saw the snarling grotesque being from some hellish dimension that had returned to threaten Timmy and their wives.

"I had to hand it to Deidre," George said. "She was grabbing a fistful of hair in one hand and punching the creature with the other. I thought Fred had lost his nerve when he turned and ran from the room, but when he returned a few minutes later, I quickly saw that he had a plan. In one hand he carried a huge flashlight with the brightest beam that I had ever seen, and in the other he held a twelve-gauge shotgun.

"He directed the beam into the monster's eyes, then fired the shotgun directly into its stomach at extremely close range."

Whether or not the demonic entity could really be harmed by the blast from a shotgun, at least the concerted acts of resistance caused it to disappear in a flash of reddish light.

In its stead, it left the most wretched, sickening odor of decay and filth imaginable.

"The stench was so foul that we were all nauseated," Tina said. "Our eyes were watering from the stink, and we could hardly breathe. We knew that none of us would be able to stay in the Seevers' lovely home that night. We may have banished the demon, but it had left a parting shot that drove us out of the house."

A week later, the Martells learned that the Seevers' beautiful lakeside home had been completely destroyed in a fire that had begun under mysterious circumstances. From what Tina and George could ascertain, the tragic fire appeared to have ended once and for all the attentions that a demon from the darkest regions of the Shadow World had directed toward Anna Delapena and, later, Deidre Seevers.

No one can know for certain why the monster had been activated in the first place. The entity may have been attracted to the young couples by the tensions of their marital adjustments and by the vibrations of the life force emanating from their sexual activity.

But why did it seem to focus its most hostile actions on Anna? Perhaps Anna had inherited a potential for psychism from her mother, Deidre, that may somehow have presented the demonic creature with a special kind of challenge. Although the phenomena in the old mansion began with somewhat ordinary poltergeistic disturbances, they quickly seemed to be fed by evil deeds that had been perpetrated in the house decades before the two couples moved in to occupy and to energize the place. Whatever the true scope of the haunting phenomena, they seem to have culminated in either the attraction of, or the creation of, a violent and malignant entity that immediately focused its rage upon Anna, and later, her mother, who tried to interfere.

To the Martells, who shared this remarkable account with me, the experiences demonstrated to them that entities that haunt one house can, if they will it, move their ghostly machinations along with the family or, in Anna's case, the unwilling center of the haunting.

CHAPTER FIVE

Frightening Encounters with Spirit Parasites

*L*angwith Junction, England 1991: A seventeen-year-old carpenter's apprentice took part in a Ouija board session at a friend's house because it looked like fun. Almost at once, he felt the presence of something incredibly evil enter the room. He began to shake uncontrollably and heard voices telling him to kill his parents and his sister. When he returned home, he lashed out at his sister and tried to strangle his mother. As the voices shouted at him, the young man flew off the floor and floated in midair. The temperature in the house became like ice as pictures on the wall spun around and furniture bounced across the room. When a summoned priest entered the home, the electric power went out and the cleric's crucifix shattered. The hellish phenomena continued for a week until a lay demonologist managed to banish the rampaging spirit parasite.

Genoa, Italy 1992: A forty-eight-year-old actress and her twenty-six-year-old daughter could not think of any reason why their penthouse apartment should suddenly have been infested with devils. Two priests tried unsuccessfully to exorcise the invading home wreckers, but furniture continued to topple over, objects hovered in midair, plates soared out of cabinets, food left the refrigerator and smeared itself on the walls, and the apartment was often filled with the suffocating odor of sulphur.

Domoszlo, Hungary 1989: For two terrible years, seventeen-year-old Tamas Nagy was tormented by a vicious entity that tumbled furniture in his presence, started fires in his home and school dormitory, and sometimes threw knives that narrowly missed him. Tamas even underwent the mysterious process of teleportation at the invisible hands of the demon. He had just finished being examined by a psychiatrist in a hospital in Budapest when, a very short time later, he appeared in a police station one hundred miles away.

Campo Grande, Brazil 1991: For several months, as many as ten mysterious fires a day suddenly erupted in the home of a night watchman and his family. Clothes in closets began to burn, furniture smoldered, mattresses and blankets caught on fire, flames even erupted on concrete floors. The fire commandant and his crew witnessed the enigmatic fires bursting into life through the home. Numerous tests were conducted to determine if there could possibly be any kind of scientific explanation for the fires. When technology failed to find the source of the hellish flames, three monks came to hold a prayer ceremony in the home. For a few days it appeared that the religious rite had been triumphant—then the accursed fires began again.

Hebron, Connecticut 1990: A thirty-five-year-old registered nurse and her young son were driven out of their 110-year-old rented Victorian home by invisible beings that she termed "evil spirits." The phenomena had begun as they were moving in and unpacking their things. A telephone in the house began to ring and ring. The nurse didn't answer the phone call from the spirit world—because they had yet to install a telephone. (When she finally did get a telephone, something kept ripping the real one out of the walls.) Lights turned themselves on and off, and the two of them constantly heard footsteps running through an upstairs hallway. And their cat was once teleported from one locked room to another.

Well-known psychical researchers Ed and Lorraine Warren were called in to investigate the haunting phenomena in the Victorian house. According to Lorraine: "We discovered a confused, frustrated human spirit centered in the [second floor] bedroom. But I also felt the presence of something evil—something inhuman and terribly dangerous. It has never walked this earth in human form, except to possess the body of another being."

More Medical Professionals Recognize Certain Physical and Mental Afflictions May Be Caused by Demons

Dramatic accounts of spirit or demonic possession come into this office from all over the world, yet whenever one begins seriously to discuss the possibility that demonic possession or spirit-parasitism may truly exist, one receives almost at once the raised eyebrow, the scoffing laughter, and the accusation that such theories push the study of mental illness back into medieval times. Nonetheless, in recent years there have been a growing number of medical doctors, psychiatrists, clinical psychologists, and members of the clergy who are becoming open-minded enough and bold enough to suggest that we might reconsider certain areas of mental health and categories of abnormal psychic states as evidence of spirit parasites.

In October 1991, my colleague Dr. Franklin R. Ruehl reported on the work of Dr. Ralph Allison, senior psychiatrist at the California state prison in San Luis Obispo, who said that in his opinion many people who appear to be mentally ill are actually possessed by the spirits of dead people or demons.

"The spirit may be that of a human being who died," Dr. Allison said, "Or it may be a spirit entity that has never been a human being and sometimes identifies itself as an agent of evil. Possession should be considered as a possible cause whenever a psychiatric subject is being evaluated."

Rediscovering the Human Soul

Researchers from many different academic disciplines have recently turned their efforts to quantifying the human soul, attempting to describe it in terms that would be more acceptable to contemporary men and women. Perhaps, as some theorists have phrased it, the soul is an electromagnetic force that holds together the protoplasmic energy that existed in a physical body prior to death. Many psychical researchers, together with the majority of religionists, perceive the soul as an exact, but invisible, duplicate of the living physical body. Some occultists call this duplicate an *astral body*.

Current modalities of the universe agree that energy can never be destroyed. Therefore, it is reasoned, even though we may discard our physical bodies at death, the soul energy that we have nourished during our lifetime on Earth exists even after we have died. At the time of death, this psychic energy force separates itself from the body and begins a new existence in a higher, spiritual dimension.

A number of parapsychologists have agreed that there may be very little difference between the seen and unseen worlds. The electromagnetic structure of the soul may continue to have the same habits, thoughts, memories, feelings, and flaws that were expressed in its physical plane existence.

Thus, if a person has spent his entire life on Earth in pursuit of sensual pleasures, the psychic soul personality will experience the same hedonistic drives after

death. He will attempt to return to all of his old, plea-
surable places. And he will undergo a traumatic shock
when he slowly realizes that he is no longer in a physical body and that none of his old companions can see
him.

According to some of these theories, the first change
in the personality of the hedonist would begin to occur
when the entity comes into contact with other souls
who have been out of the body for a longer period of
time. Many of these souls will have elevated themselves to a higher plane of awareness. With the assistance of these more advanced souls and with the
guidance of angelic Light Beings, all of the entity's
spiritual problems can be worked out in time. All
physical concerns will fade into irrelevance. Sensual
memories of the previous material existence will be
forgotten.

Renegade and Restless Spirits

But once in a while something goes wrong. In certain instances a discarnate spirit retains its free will to
act as it chooses. Perhaps the entity had worked hard
in life but had not yet attained its goal before physical
death. It may have been handicapped by an emotional
or physical problem. Maybe death came too quickly in
the form of an unexpected accident.

Consider the tremendous, unresolved shock when
someone dies unexpectedly and enters the spirit world.
And if there were additional negative factors, such as
a bitter dispute left unsettled, an old score left unpaid,

an argument left unresolved, then that restless spirit might hunger to return to the physical world in order to obtain vengeance.

Such a renegade spirit will refuse to allow the natural order of time to ease its pain and anger. It will wish desperately to return to the world of the living. It will set about resolving its dissatisfaction by parasitism. The disembodied spirit will seek to attach itself to the physical body of a living human being. Humans are most susceptible to invasion by spirit entities when they are fatigued and exhausted; when they have undergone a period of severe stress; when they are emotionally upset or very angry; and when they are under the influence of drugs, alcohol, or any other mind-altering substances.

Spirit Parasites Attack Those at a Low Ebb, Emotionally or Physically

Certain parapsychologists who have specialized in such areas of research have begun to speak out in grim warnings that mental slavery to a spirit parasite may be commonplace. Professor Ian Currie of Toronto's Guelph University concluded that such entities take over the minds of people who are emotionally or physically at a low ebb.

"The beings seem able to leech on those people because they had been weakened by strains and stresses with which they could not cope," he said. "I have come across many cases of discarnate entities who wanted to make humans their slaves. These spirits are real, make no mistake."

Dr. Wilson Van Dusen, who served as chief psychologist at Mendocino State Hospital and lectured at the University of California at Davis, has studied the problem of spirit possession extensively, dealing with thousands of patients during his years as a clinical psychologist, and authoring one hundred fifty scientific papers and several books on the subject. According to Dr. Van Dusen's conclusions, these demons can "find a weak point of conscience and work on it interminably. They invade every nook and cranny of privacy; work on every weakness and credibility; claim awesome powers; lie, make promises, and then undermine the patient's will."

A spirit parasite can seize the controlling mechanism of its host body and direct the enslaved human to perform harmful actions involving alcohol, drugs, and promiscuous sex. Once the spirit parasite has attached itself to a living human, the "split" personality of the schizophrenic may be observed. A campaign of harassment might be launched against a human enemy of the spirit parasite. It might control the host body to punch someone in the nose, and the baffled human might never understand why he has started a fight with a total stranger. The spirit parasite might even implant murderous thoughts in a host's mind and direct the enslaved human to kill its enemies who are still in the physical world. Then, once the crime has been committed, the parasite may withdraw back to the spiritual dimension, leaving the poor, confused human alone, charged with murder, while the true assassin has escaped.

Dr. Van Dusen once reflected that human lives may only be the little free space at the confluence of giant higher and lower spiritual hierarchies. "There is some kind of lesson in this," he concluded. "Man, freely poised between good and evil, under the influence of cosmic forces he usually doesn't know exist. Man, thinking he chooses, may be the resultant of other forces."

A Checklist of Demonic Traits

My wife, Sherry Hansen Steiger, is an ordained Protestant minister, who has learned to take very seriously the fact that one of the most important aspects of Jesus's ministry on Earth was the casting out of demons, the spiritual parasites that had invaded the bodies and minds of the innocent. Some years ago, after many requests for such guidelines, Sherry drew up the following checklist of demonic traits:

Demons . . .

- are spiritual entities without physical bodies.
- roam the Earth seeking to torment whoever attracts them.
- have supernatural powers.
- are numerous and organized.
- can inflict sickness and mental disorders on their victims.
- can possess or control humans and animals.
- lie and deceive.

- Teach false and misleading spiritual doctrines.
- oppose all positive teachings and actions.
- tremble before the invocation of God.
- respect the name and power of Jesus and other spiritual teachers.

A Nurse Battles a Spirit Parasite for a Patient's Soul

One of the most dramatic cases of possession by a spirit parasite that I have ever heard was provided to me by Caroline Spencer, a nurse who specializes in private care. In 1969, she received a job offer from a young businessman whose wife had become crippled in a hunting accident. The couple had no children, and the wife was lonely, as well as in need of professional care.

"Meg is an absolute saint," Peter Eston told Caroline over the telephone. "She never complains. There'll be a maid, Mrs. Cromwell, there until around five each afternoon. She'll take care of the cooking, of course, and any cleaning that needs to be done."

When Caroline Spencer arrived at the Eston residence, she was aware that Peter Eston had already left on a three-day business trip. Since it was around five-thirty, she knew also that Mrs. Cromwell would have left, but that there would be dinner being kept warm in the oven.

She let herself in with the key that had been sent to her by Peter Eston, and she found Mrs. Eston in her bedroom. Propped up in bed against two large purple satin pillows, Meg Eston's long blonde hair framed her beautiful face and gave her an overall angelic aura of tranquility and beauty. Caroline was, therefore, completely unprepared for the welcome that she received from her patient.

"Good evening, Caroline, baby," Meg Eston greeted her, a strange smile stretching her lips in what almost appeared to be a leer. "Oh, I am certain that we are going to get along just fine."

Caroline Spencer writes in her report of her experience how surprised she was at the rather crude familiarity displayed by Meg Eston upon their first meeting.

> I asked Mrs. Eston how she knew my first name, since I always wished to keep things on as professional a basis as possible with my clients. She told me that she knew lots of things about me. This puzzled me, because Mr. Eston and I had not exchanged information of any personal matter. I should have noticed then that Mrs. Eston's eyes had a strange cast to them. There almost seemed to be a flame flickering behind each of them. I excused myself and went to the kitchen to begin serving dinner to Mrs. Eston on the elaborate wooden tray that stretched across her queen-size bed.

Caroline recalled that she put in an exhausting first night in the Eston household. Every few minutes, Mrs. Eston would summon her to her bedside on the weakest of pretexts, then complain loudly about the nurse's general incompetence.

When Caroline suggested that they should both get some sleep, Meg Eston laughed and told her, "I don't need any sleep—and you, my dear, are not going to get any!"

The next morning when Mrs. Cromwell arrived, Caroline hoped that she might get some rest. The maid, a stout woman in her mid-fifties, introduced herself to Caroline, then assessed her condition bluntly. "You look worn out, sweetheart. Weren't you able to sleep well in a strange bed?"

When the nurse sighed and explained that she had been up all night with a demanding patient, Mrs. Cromwell arched an eyebrow and studied her carefully in several moments of skeptical silence. "You can't be talking about Mrs. Eston. That woman is a saint. I've never heard her complain about a single thing. Did she have the flu or something?"

"Something," Caroline answered, hopefully not too sharply. If Peter Eston and Mrs. Cromwell considered Meg Eston's behavior in the saint category, she would hate to see what they would deem bad behavior.

I couldn't wait to meet Peter Eston in person and give him a piece of my mind. So his wife was a saint, eh? So she never complained? Somehow the woman had certainly fooled her husband and her day maid. I decided to call Mrs. Eston's doctor and arrange for some tranquilizers or sleep aids for her so that I could get some rest that night. When I explained briefly Mrs. Eston's behavior of the night before, he expressed his amazement but said that he would stop by right after lunch on his way to do rounds at the hospital.

The nurse had no sooner cradled the receiver when she heard a deep male voice singing an obscene song. She knew that Mrs. Cromwell had gone to the market to buy some fresh vegetables and that she was alone in the house with Mrs. Eston.

Caroline put a weary hand to her throbbing forehead. She could now tell that the coarse voice was coming from Mrs. Eston's room. Had the beautiful "saint" taken herself a vulgar lover to while away the long hours in bed? Although the accident had surely crippled her, there was no question that Meg Eston remained a breathtakingly attractive woman, albeit a bit emaciated. For a terrible moment, Caroline Spencer feared that she might be losing her mind.

The deep, foul voice was coming from Mrs. Eston's own throat. "So you called the doctor, huh?" the gutteral voice said harshly. "You're a little tattletale, honey, but you are going to be in for a surprise."

When the doctor arrived, Mrs, Eston was completely composed, and she spoke in cultured, well-modulated tones. She was sweet, pleasant, the very picture of the ideal long-suffering patient.

The doctor stopped for a cup of coffee with me before he left. I wanted to mention the coarse, vulgar tone and language that Mrs. Eston had been using moments before he arrived, but I could tell from his manner that I was the one under analysis. He tried to make the conversation about medical schools and courses of study sound casual and shop-talkish, but I knew that he was really sounding me out about my experience and background. Behind his pleasant, professional smile, he was questioning my qualifications as a private nurse. Before he left, he told me that he could see no reason to prescribe tranquilizers for Mrs. Eston. When I began to argue my reasons, he became very brusque, and his manner as he left the house suggested that I could benefit more than Meg Eston from such a prescription.

Caroline went to her room and lay down on the bed. She had roughly three hours before Mrs. Cromwell left. Without bothering to remove her uniform, she rolled over on her side and fell into a deep sleep.

Fortunately, the maid didn't bother to check out with me before she left and when the deep, howling voice awakened me, I saw by my wristwatch that it was nearly six-thirty. A foul angry voice was screaming that it wanted to eat. It wondered where the lazy bitch of a nurse was.

I walked to Mrs. Eston's bedroom and looked deep into the black, glittering eyes. "Why do you say such terrible things, Mrs. Eston?" That was all that I could manage, and the strange, hostile woman laughed and mocked me for my weakness.

For another wretched night, Caroline Spencer bore the curses and imprecations of the deep voice that boomed from within the frail, crippled woman.

Once when she was attempting to bathe her, Mrs. Eston's hand shot out to grasp her by the throat. Caroline nearly blacked out before she managed to wrest the powerful fingers from her throat.

"You're stronger than you look," the deep voice growled approvingly, as the nurse sat gasping on the floor. "You're hard to wear down, too. How are you in bed, honey? Got a lot of stamina in the sack? Can you show a man a good time? Baby, if I could just get these damn legs working, I would sure as hell find out how good you are!"

Caroline looked up in horror at the black eyes that looked down on her with such evil, yet sensual, appraisal. She began to consider quite strongly that the accident had somehow splintered Meg Eston's psyche. Perhaps she was dealing with schizophrenia or a split personality—the saint and the devil.

When the word "devil" crossed my thoughts, it seemed unconsciously to trigger some old concepts from my very religious childhood that had been banished years ago by my scientific training. Dimly, in the farthest reaches of my mind, I began to think about possession, about evil spirits, demons—

creatures that I had rejected as products of superstitious minds long, long ago.

Eerily, as if Mrs. Eston could read my mind, she laughed and then said pointedly, "Ah, are you beginning to get the picture now, honey? Meg Eston, hell! To hell with Meg Eston! You come close to me again, sugar, and you'll find out who I really am!"

Caroline got to her feet and left the room. She thought again of calling Mrs. Eston's physician and demanding that he come at once to view his saintly patient as she really was. But at the same time, she now realized that by the time he arrived, Mrs. Eston would be the sweet, smiling angelic being that had deceived her maid, her husband, and everyone except her nurse.

Later that night, the foul voice stopped shouting selections from what seemed to be an inexhaustible supply of filthy songs, jokes, and assorted vulgarities. Caroline was astonished to hear the sound of soft weeping coming from Mrs. Eston's room. Suspecting a trap, she slowly entered the room and discovered her patient in a state of confusion.

"Who . . . who are you?" Meg Eston wondered as Caroline approached her bedside. "Are you my nurse?"

Caroline nodded and sat down beside her patient.

"Where's my husband? Where's Peter?"

Caroline explained that he was away on business but due to return on the next evening.

"I'm so afraid," Mrs. Eston said. "What's happening

to me? Oh, nurse, whoever you are, please keep that horrid, ugly brute away from me!"

Caroline took advantage of the lull to feed Mrs. Eston some soup and to complete her sponge bath. She talked soothingly to the woman, and when she left her patient so that they might both get a good night's sleep, she allowed the terrible thought to escape from the corner of her brain where she had been keeping it chained: *Meg Eston was possessed.*

If Caroline had yearned for rest that night, there was none to be had. She had just lain down when she heard Mrs. Eston vomiting.

"No food for you, bitch!" roared the deep voice over and over again in between the sounds of the woman retching. "And no rest for you until I stop your heart and send you to hell!"

The nurse ran to the woman with cold cloths, but she was given no opportunity to soothe Meg Eston's torment or to clean up the mess.

"Let her lie in filth and vomit," the hoarse voice told her. "Let her *die* in filth and vomit. You come closer to help the bitch, and I'll wring your silly neck!"

"I know what you are now," Caroline said defiantly. "And with God's help, I'll do my duty."

•

I had not been in church for years, but I still prayed and felt that I was a spiritual person. All I can say now is that it must have been the Holy Spirit that entered me that night. I talked on about God's love and God's goodness. I talked about how God answered prayers. Whatever the terrible thing was that had entered Mrs. Eston, it clamped her palms to her head and screamed that it would not listen to such talk. But I talked on and on until, glory be, she collapsed back on the bed and lay quietly. I took advantage of the quiet time to clean up the vomit that had spewed out of the poor woman.

When Peter Eston returned that next evening, he took one look at Caroline Spencer's haggard appearance and knew that his worst fears had been realized. He begged the nurse's forgiveness. "I thought . . . I hoped Meg might be different for you. I knew that if I told you her true condition, you probably wouldn't have taken the job."

At Caroline's prompting, he told her how they had found his wife's body lying inside an old stone hut on the day of the hunting accident. No one could ever understand why she had gone into the hut and how an accomplished sportswoman such as she had accidentally shot herself. The only feasible theory that they had developed was that Meg had set her shotgun against a wall and it had slipped off the moist rock and gone off when it had struck the floor. The pellets had damaged her spine and had rendered her paralyzed from the waist down.

The nature of the hut? Nothing special, just an old stone house where some nutty old recluse had lived and died hating all humankind.

"And now," Peter Eston said, fighting to hold back tears, "my poor wife, my beautiful, talented, accomplished wife has been transformed by the accident into some kind of lunatic. How that damned, deep, foul voice comes out of her, I'll never understand."

At almost the same instant, the nurse and her client realized that it had become silent in his wife's room. Caroline told the anxious husband that she would check on things.

"I shall never forget that sight," Caroline Spencer wrote in her report to me.

I have seen death in many manifestations, but I pray I shall never again see the equal of what I saw in that room. Mrs. Eston's facial features had become distorted into an expression of malignant evil. The face lying on that silk pillow resembled that of a gargoyle or some hideous demon. Somehow I steeled myself to check for pulse and respiration. There was none. The poor woman was at last at peace.

I returned to Mr. Eston and told him that he absolutely should not enter the bedroom. Somehow I managed to convince him that he would never recognize the once-beautiful features of his wife in the creature that now lay on the bed.

Later I learned that Meg Eston had been buried quietly in a closed-casket funeral. The mortician had worked for several hours on her face, but her features continued to slip back into that horrible grimace. Whatever had possessed Meg Eston had won a physical victory. I only pray that it had not been able to claim her soul as well as her body.

A Pattern Profile of Those Possessed by a Spirit Parasite

If someone you know has demonstrated a dramatic alteration in personal behavior and you are certain that he or she does not abuse drugs and has no previous history of mental problems, that person may have been invaded by a spirit parasite. Consult with a physician, a psychologist, or a psychiatrist and consider possession by a spirit parasite as one of many possible diagnoses. Those who suffer from invasion by an uninvited entity from Shadow World may begin to manifest such changes in personality or personal behavior as the following:

- They may begin to hear voices directing them to perform acts they never before even considered.
- They may frequently see the image of the spirit parasite as it existed in its physical life as a human—or, in the case of a nonhuman entity, as it truly appears in its demonic countenance.
- In the weeks and months that follow, they may fall into states of blacked-out consciousness, times of which they later have absolutely no memory.
- On occasions, sometimes in the midst of conversations, their conscious minds may be blocked and a trancelike state will come over them.
- They may be observed to be walking differently, speaking in a different tone and manner, and acting in strange, irrational ways.

- They may begin doing things that they have never done before. Friends and family will remark that they are behaving like totally different people.
- In the very worst cases, the parasite being will consume their life. The evil spell may reach a climax with the possessed committing murder, suicide, or some violent antisocial act.

Protect Yourself from Spirit Parasites

Remember that spirit parasites cannot achieve power over you unless you somehow invite them into your private space or unless they are attracted to you by negative thoughts and actions. You will become especially susceptible to such spirit invasion if you should abuse alcohol or drugs or exploit someone mentally or physically.

Never enter either meditation or prayer with the sole thought of obtaining personal aggrandizement or ego satisfaction. Selfish motivations may risk your becoming easily affected by those discordant spirits who wish to entrap you as their slave. Adopting a negative attitude toward life in general—and toward those around you in particular—will also attract spirit parasites to your dark spiritual vibrations. Realize that evil or negativity is an imbalanced, chaotic, destructive energy, the opposite of growth and productivity. When you are negative, depressed, and discordant, you place yourself right in the path of a spirit parasite from the lower frequencies of Shadow World.

Beware of exploring the occult world of Tarot, Ouija, spirit mediumship, and so forth. Without the proper discipline, study, and discernment, you will be liable to interact only with those entities who will seek to deceive you and entrap you. Such tools of the occult should never be utilized by any student other than those who have learned a firm sort of mind control and the techniques of surrounding themselves with loving and harmonious vibrations.

If you should seek contact with higher intelligences, remember always that our physical world is closer to the realm of the lower, more negative spiritual frequencies of Shadow World than it is to the dimension of the most harmonious beings. Because we exist in a material world, our psyches will always contain more aspects similar to those of the lower vibratory realm than the higher spiritual planes.

If you should have an encounter with a spirit being from the chaotic regions of Shadow World, you will quite likely experience a prickling sensation that will seem to crawl over your entire body. You will instantly be filled with an awareness that you have entered into a very dangerous liaison. If you continue the contact, you will experience a mounting sense of terror or a distinct sensation of unease, depending upon the strength of the discordant vibrations emanating from the spirit parasite. If you should find yourself seemingly locked into such an encounter, utter prayers of love and harmony and ask that angelic guidance be manifested around you.

Understand that the Shadow World houses all manner of discordant spirits as well as more benevolent and benign entities. Be aware of the fact that the troubled spirits will continue their contentious ways beyond physical death, and they will often attempt to influence the minds, and therefore the lives, of those who will receive them. Also be very aware that many of the inhabitants of Shadow World have never been human. Some envy your flesh and your soul. Others hold you in the greatest contempt.

Keep always in mind that the best way to avoid a negative encounter with a spirit parasite is to seek to elevate your thoughts, works, and deeds to the highest levels. Endeavor to walk in harmony with the Oneness of all creation and on the path of the Master of Life. When your purpose is that of the angels, you will attract the attention only of those entities who exist in the realm of the highest spiritual vibrations. You will not have to fear encountering the spirit parasites and the negative entities of Shadow World, for you will receive only meaningful, inspirational contact with the benevolent beings of the highest order.

CHAPTER SIX

The Enigma of Spirit Mimics

There is one type of being that issues forth from Shadow World whose true purpose is extremely enigmatic. On occasion, they play the role of the good Samaritan, the angelic guardians. In other instances, they appear to be entities who wish to impersonate men and women in order to experience the full range of human emotions, especially those of love and companionship. And then there are those more distasteful encounters, when these entities behave in ways that are mischievous, bordering on cruel. I have come to term these entities Spirit Mimics, for they generally do excellent impersonations of us humans. For quite a period of time, these mimics can do a remarkably good job of fooling the men and women with whom they have chosen to interact.

If one of these spirit impressionists should choose to impersonate a friend or family member, you would soon begin to notice a number of very subtle, but very important, differences between the imposter and your friend or loved one. These spirit mimics talk like us, act like us, dress like us, and they can even feign very convincing emotional responses. Once again, however, it's the little things that give them away.

Very often, their manner of dress is inappropriate. Another clue lies in their use of language, which is very often dated with vernacular expressions and jargon from an earlier time. Some people have also reported that their facial expressions are not always in sync with the attitudes or emotions that they are ostensibly vocalizing. And for some humans who have nearly fallen victim to a Spirit Mimic, the entity was given away by its eyes. "If eyes are the window to the soul," one correspondent told me, "then when I looked into her eyes, regardless of how beautiful they were, there really didn't seem to be anybody home inside."

He Will Remember Nara Forever

Cary, a freelance writer from New York, began his account of a strange interaction with a Spirit Mimic by explaining that in the spring of 1992 he was called back to Prescott, Arizona, to be at the bedside of his dying father. After his father had passed on, he was left with a number of legal affairs which he needed to attend to, such as the closing of his father's estate and the settling of bills.

My mother and sister had been killed in an automobile accident outside of Phoenix in 1984. I had
not lived in Prescott since 1981, and I saw no reason
to return now that Dad had died. He had a number
of good insurance policies, so most of the hospital
and medical bills would be paid. I put the house up
for sale after the reading of Dad's will. As his only
surviving heir, he left me a considerable amount of
money that would permit me to get a better apartment back in New York, and buy me the time I
needed to finish my novel without having to inter-
rupt the narrative flow with quick cash assignments
for magazines.

While he was going through his parents' things in
the house where he had spent his childhood and
teenage years, Cary became morose. Sorting through
old photographs of the various stages of the family's
growth filled him with nostalgia; seeing pictures of his
sister Andrea brought tears to his eyes. He set about
boxing a good many family pictures to ship back to the
city where he would one day find the time to place
them all in a scrapbook. He called a number of Good-
will stores and Salvation Army outlets to pick up the
furniture and the clothes that filled the closets; but
with every errand he ran to dispose of his parents' and
sister's lifetime of personal treasures, he found himself
becoming more and more depressed and saddened.
He knew that unless he somehow managed to elevate
his mood, it would be impossible to return to his
apartment and begin work on the novel.

Then it dawned on him that he was thirty-four, single, unattached, and he suddenly had some money. He could afford to travel a bit and reestablish some mental balance before he returned to work.

Cary had always loved the red rock area around Sedona long before it became a haven for New Agers with their crystals seeking vortexes to energize their psyches. He decided to spend a few days there, maybe take a couple of Jeep tours to some of the new archaeological sites.

One day I drove out on the airport road, pulled over to the side, and walked to a spot that my parents used to take Andrea and me to when we were kids. I knew that the New Agers had declared this spot one of the supposed hot vortexes, but I just wanted to see the spectacular view once again and remember some of the good times that we had had as a family when I was a kid. And that was where I met Nara.

The young woman was meditating on a ledge that looked out over the picturesque valley. Cary found her to be as breathtakingly beautiful as the rest of the natural scenery at the vortex. Her long black hair was braided and the two strands reached nearly to her waist. She wore a white buckskin shirt and faded blue jeans. Her lovely features were serene as she quietly searched within. For a long time, Cary remembered, the only sounds he heard were the beating of his heart, a gentle wind blowing through the pine boughs, and the call of a hawk high overhead.

I know this sounds ridiculously romantic, but it truly seemed as though she was waiting there for me to arrive. I sat off to her side for what seemed like hours before she opened her large brown eyes and smiled at me. She said that her name was Nara, and she invited me to join her on the ledge. We sat there and talked until sunset. It was as if I had known her all my life.

They had dinner that night at one of the new Mexican restaurants in Sedona, and later that evening, they spent the first of many nights together in Nara's cabin near Oak Creek Canyon. Cary's "few days" in Sedona multiplied into a few weeks, then a few months.

Nara became my reason for existence. I was completely in love with her. Night and day for three months I saw nothing in my universe but Nara. I sent my landlord monthly checks to keep my apartment in New York, and I begged Nara to return to the city and marry me. My friend Ray forwarded mail from my editors, but I tossed them into the wastebasket. Writing magazine articles seemed like something I had done in another lifetime, and the concept of the novel that I had been working on for nearly two years was fading from my memory. Nara was giving me a fresh, new inspiration, and I burned with the idea for a work of fiction that would be filled with my passion for her.

Whenever Cary brought up the subject of marriage and Nara's returning with him to New York City, Nara would only smile and say that she was an Arizona girl.

"My people have lived here for generations," she would tell him. "My soul is made up of the mountains, the desert, the red rocks of Sedona. I am one with my Arizona."

Cary would argue that he, too, was an Arizona boy—but she would learn to love the excitement of the big city with its massive concrete canyons. Not to mention the theaters, the museums, the libraries, the restaurants.

But Nara would only laugh and say that all the excitement she needed was in the land of her people. And if he would stay with her there, she would never want for anything.

I was always puzzled by her references to "her people," for although judging by her appearance she could certainly have been Native American, she denied any tribal connections. She would only say that she very much admired the native people. This was certainly in evidence by her frequent playing of tapes of Native American music, especially the haunting flute music of Carlos Nakai.

After nearly four months spent in the almost otherworldly haven of Nara's cabin in the lovely natural environment of Oak Creek Canyon, Cary decided that he really must return to New York to maintain at least a few of his editorial connections and to check on his apartment. The world of the greater reality had begun to intrude on his sojourn in paradise. He promised to call Nara every day and to return as soon as possible.

Nara seemed amazingly stoical about his leaving. Only when he got in the rental car to drive to the Phoenix airport did she permit a lone tear to escape from a corner of one of her large brown eyes.

As soon as I reached my apartment in New York, I called Nara. I was baffled when a recording came on that informed me that I had not reached a working number. Even though I was exhausted from the flight and the long taxi ride into the city, I tried a dozen times before I gave up. I didn't want Nara to worry about me, and I grew increasingly frustrated at my inability to reach her.

After three days of receiving nothing but the same maddening recording, Cary decided to fly back to Arizona at once, and he pressed his friend Ray into accompanying him.

As weird as this will seem, I drove back and forth on the blacktop that winds around Oak Creek Canyon, and I could not find the dirt road that led to Nara's cabin. Ray kept looking at me like I was totally nuts. How could it be that I couldn't find the place where I had spent most of the past four months? I finally got him to hike with me back into the woods until I found an old, broken-down, moss-covered cabin where I thought Nara's home had to be.

Cary felt as though he were having a nervous breakdown—or that he really was going nuts.

At first Ray teased him about not being able to find the cabin. "You should have sprinkled bread crumbs," he said, laughing. "You sure ain't no Davy Crockett, man."

By the end of the second day when they could find no one who really knew Nara or where she lived, Ray had stopped joking. But as they canvassed their favorite haunts in Sedona, everyone with whom they spoke—the waiters and waitresses, the shopkeepers, the tour guides, the clerks in the post office, the attendants at the gas station—remembered the beautiful dark-haired girl who had been with Cary for the fourteen weeks that he had lived there.

My mind kept searching for some rational explanation for Nara's disappearance, but I could not come up with any theory that made any kind of sense. We returned to New York, completely baffled and confused. Ray was incredibly supportive, and I would have totally collapsed without his genuine friendship.

Once I got back to my apartment, I went into a complete depression. I didn't even leave the place for weeks. By the time I managed to beat back some of the gloom, the empty boxes of delivered food were thickly scattered throughout my entire apartment.

It was almost a year later, Cary said, when he was sitting in his apartment with Ray and his friend Brooke, discussing writing, philosophy, the latest theater openings—and, of course, Nara. He simply could not get the beautiful woman out of his mind. The conversation at every gathering—whether in a restaurant, bar, or Cary's apartment—his friends patiently understood, would eventually lead to his lost love, Nara.

A few minutes after midnight, there was a knock at my door, and when I opened it, I was astonished beyond speech to see my darling Nara suddenly standing before me. She was beautiful and serene, seemingly amused by my surprise and confusion. She was dressed in her familiar white buckskin, but black slacks had replaced her customary jeans. She came into my arms, and we embraced passionately, entering the room in a kind of mad dance of love.

When Ray and Brooke realized that this was my lost love Nara, they demonstrated the greatest consideration and left us alone after they had expressed their joy at meeting her at last. Although they remained but a few discreet moments to chat with Nara, I could see that she had completely captivated them.

Of course Cary wanted to know what had happened to her and where she had been for so long, but whenever he asked such questions, she would place a gentle finger on his lips and remind him that she was now there with him.

"Let's not waste a moment," she told him. "There will be time for questions and answers later. The most important thing is that I am here with you now."

When they went to bed that night, Cary remembers that he held Nara tightly, as if he were fearful that she might suddenly vanish.

Once, much later in the night, he reached out for her and was reassured by her presence. She lay propped up on an elbow, her large brown eyes gazing at him with love and kindness. "Why do you sleep so restlessly, my darling?" she asked.

Cary answered frankly, expressing his deepest fear. "Because I am afraid that if I go to sleep, you are going to vanish. You will disappear again. I have that terrible feeling."

Nara laughed at his fears. "Go to sleep, my love. Go to sleep."

But when Cary awakened the next morning, Nara, his dearest love, was gone.

> The pillow still held the shape of her dear head, but she was gone, just as I feared she would be. And somehow I knew that I would never see Nara again—whatever she really was, a woman, a ghost, a nature sprite, an angel, or something not yet understood by mere mortals.

Cary said that he had been to Sedona twice after Nara disappeared, visiting all their favorite haunts, talking to acquaintances that they had made and those people who had known of their love. From all he can learn, Nara has never been seen there again. In concluding his bizarre account, Cary stated,

I might believe that I was crazy and imagined Nara and our love affair, but I at least have the testimonies of Ray and Brooke, who saw Nara with their own eyes. I also have a statement from the maintenance man in my building who remembers seeing a dark-haired woman in a white buckskin shirt standing in front of my apartment just before she started knocking on the door. In spite of these testimonies and the kindnesses of my friends, I shall undoubtedly be haunted by the memory of Nara for the rest of my life.

From the human perspective, Nara, whoever or whatever she truly was, seems cruel. To inspire such great love from a man, disappear for many months, then reappear only to engage him in a farewell night of lovemaking seems extremely perplexing to those of us with human emotions. What was Nara's purpose in establishing a relationship with Cary? What did she gain from their interaction as lovers? Was it her intention merely to explore the sensations and emotions of human love? Was this a game to Nara, or did she have a much more serious purpose, a plan that is presently beyond our mortal ken?

Certain colleagues of mine with whom I previously shared this story, have suggested that Nara is like the succubi of old, those female demons who appear to make love to mortal men. But Cary describes her as far too gentle and genuinely affectionate when they were together to think seriously of her being a succubus.

Other researchers of the paranormal have theorized that Nara was an alien, seeking Cary's seed in order to create a hybrid race in some secret underground base or mother ship. This theory also seems very unlikely, for if gathering Cary's sperm was Nara's only motive in establishing a relationship with him, then she need not have stayed with him as long as she did. Plus the fact that Cary revealed in confidence that they had always practiced safe sex. Nara would have insisted upon unprotected sex if it were her goal to become pregnant.

I have always found it fascinating to observe that how the Spirit Mimics conduct themselves depends in large part on the percipient with whom they choose to interact. Cry out in fear, and sometimes they will give you good reason to fear them. Reach out in love, as Cary did, and, at least for a time, they will return your love.

Sometimes it is not always clear what the Spirit Mimics really have in mind.

A Spirit Mimic Tried to Romance His Girlfriend

Jerry Levesque told me that during a two-week period in 1997, his girlfriend, Kelly Howard, received a number of telephone calls from someone she believed to be him.

"Fortunately, because we were going steady, I had occasion to call Kelly in between calls from this imposter," Levesque said. "I say 'fortunately,' because he usually asked Kelly to meet him in some lonely place, and fortunately because of what we later learned about this other me."

The first time that Kelly received a call from the Jerry wannabe, he asked her to meet him at a local restaurant as quickly as possible. She was getting ready and would soon have left her apartment when Jerry knocked on her door. She was puzzled when she opened the door to admit him.

"Plans change?" she asked, rushing back into the bathroom to continue putting on her makeup.

Jerry had come directly from his job at the dry cleaners, and he had stopped by to see if Kelly wanted to take in an early movie. Since they had no plans for the evening, Jerry wanted to know what plans she had in mind.

"I suppose you didn't call me twenty minutes ago and ask me to meet you at Jigg's restaurant as quickly as possible?" Kelly frowned, unable to see the humor in Jerry's peculiar manner.

When he adamantly denied making such a call, they assumed it was some friend trying to pull a prank on them. So they laughed it off and went to the movies.

The next evening, however, when Kelly knew Jerry would be working very late, she answered the telephone and heard her boyfriend's familiar voice. According to her, the conversation went like this.

Jerry: "Where were you last night?"

Kelly: "With you, silly!"

Jerry: "I waited at Jigg's for hours, but you didn't come."

Kelly: "Okay, Jerry. Cut it out. Let's not go through that again."

Jerry: "Don't get sassy with me, you little twit!"

Kelly: "Pardon me! What did you call me?"

Jerry: "A twit! That's what you are. When I tell you to be—"

At that point, as Jerry had begun to rage, Kelly hung up the telephone. It was only after she had calmed down that she began to play back the rude conversation in her mind. Twit? Where had Jerry come up with that one? The more she analyzed the whole weird telephone call, the less it really sounded like Jerry's voice.

Kelly picked up the phone and called Jerry at work. She knew Mr. Baker didn't like Jerry to receive personal calls at work, especially when they were putting in overtime, but she considered this an emergency. Jerry nervously came to the phone, gently remonstrating with her for calling him at the dry cleaners when he was on overtime. He laughed ironically when she asked if he had called her apartment earlier that night: "You're kidding, right? If I don't get off the phone right now, old man Baker will have a seizure."

Kelly was satisfied that it hadn't been Jerry on the telephone calling her a twit. But two hours later when the telephone rang again, she wasn't quite so certain.

"Meet me out by Miller's Pond, near the old mill," Jerry said.

"It's late," Kelly protested. "And you must be tired working such long hours overtime."

"I suppose that I am a bit fagged," Jerry responded. "But seeing you will wake me up."

Kelly began to snicker at the unfamiliar expression. For a young American woman in the 1990s, any form of the word "fag" made reference to homosexuality. "'Fagged!'" she echoed, then added in mock accusation: "What were you and old man Baker doing in that laundry after hours to get 'fagged'?"

Jerry was very quiet. "Why . . . as you suggested. I'm fagged, ah, you know, fatigued, exhausted from such hard work."

Kelly was hearing the warning buzzer go off in her mind. Once again, this could not be the real Jerry Levesque on the phone. "Whoever you are," she said calmly, keeping her voice even and under control, "leave me alone."

The voice at the other end pleaded with her. "Please. If you will not meet me at Miller's Pond, at least come down to the corner and speak with me."

She knew that she may have been acting foolishly, but Kelly gave the voice a "maybe."

According to her account of the incident:

I kept watching the corner for any sign of a man I might suppose was the person pretending to be Jerry on the telephone. I know I was taking a risk, but I wanted to get all these weird things resolved. If it was a friend of ours playing a joke, I would give him a piece of my mind before Jerry gave him a lump with his fist. Amazingly, around midnight, I saw Jerry—my Jerry—walk slowly up to the street corner in front of my apartment building and look up at my window. He waved and smiled, and I waved and got my sweater.

When I got about six feet away from him, I stopped and looked at him very carefully. He did look an awful lot like Jerry, but he was wearing some kind of heavy work boots, a baseball cap, and a brown leather jacket, kind of like the type I've seen in old movies that pilots wore in World War II. When I commented about the heavy boots, he said that I knew that he had just come from work. I commented that the laundry business must be getting tougher.

He reached out his hand and asked me to come with him. The light from the streetlamp was fairly bright, and I could clearly see that, except for the way he was dressed, he certainly did look like Jerry Levesque.

But then I said, "Jerry, you always told me you hated to wear baseball caps," and he took off the cap. This imposter had a crewcut, a hairstyle that Jerry Levesque would not have in a million years. I shouted at him, "So you think I'm a twit do you?" And I started to run back into the apartment building. At that same moment, Jerry—the real Jerry—pulled up in his car next to the imposter. What happened next, though unbelievable, really did happen. The phony Jerry let out a high-pitched scream and literally disappeared.

"Whatever this thing really was," Jerry Levesque said, "it tried to contact Kelly just once more, about five days later. Kelly thought for sure she was talking to me until 'I' asked her to drive out to the park and meet me for a picnic after work. The park is four miles out of town, and Kelly knew that I knew that her car was in the garage for a few days. She screamed at the false Jerry to leave her alone and never to call again. And, thank the Lord, he never did."

Neither Jerry nor Kelly have any theory to offer as to why this Spirit Mimic wished to appear as him or why it was so persistent in attempting to pursue her. One immediate response to their bizarre encounter with the entities from Shadow World is that they soon became engaged and were married four months later. In terms of a long term effect, the experience has affected them permanently in at least two ways: They will always be cautious in meeting new people, doing their best to determine if the strangers truly are who they represent themselves to be; and in their own relationship, they will always be totally honest with one another so that no interloper could ever separate them or confuse them with lies.

A Spirit Mimic Declares Their Relationship to Humans

Kent Grondahl, a graduate student at a major midwestern university, may have received some kind of clue to the identity of at least some of the Spirit Mimics from Shadow World.

"I am of Scandinavian descent and I attended a small college in Iowa that had a large number of Scandinavian-American students on campus," Grondahl began in his story of an encounter with Spirit Mimics. "One day I was out driving in the country, trying my best to clear my brain and prepare for an important test in economics the next afternoon. I was worried big time about the results, because stupidly I had been more or less erratic in my attendance in this class, and I couldn't afford a low mark on this exam."

Grondahl was very aware of the significance of this small college town in the history of Scandinavian immigration in the 1880s, and he knew that a lot of the old villages surrounding the larger community still maintained many of the Old Country customs. "I drove through this tiny village that presently supported a kind of general store, a gas station, a couple other buildings of indeterminate use, and lots of apparently deserted business locations. However, on the outskirts of the village, there appeared to be some kind of celebration going on. I heard polka music and saw a small crowd of people playing games and lining up beside what appeared to be a generous smorgasbord table."

The college student couldn't resist pulling his car over to the side of the road, getting out, and walking over to the cheery partygoers. "But suddenly my way was blocked by this big bruiser who glared at me with ice-cold eyes," Grondahl said. "He seemed to have hated me all of his life the moment he saw me. I thought he was going to punch me."

And then a tall, smiling man stepped between the brute and the student. "Svald, relax. Go back and fill your plate again," the interloper told the big man. Then turning his full attention to Grondahl, he introduced himself as Erik Hagen and inquired of him his full name. "Kent Lars Grondahl," the student answered.

Then, according to Grondahl's account:

> Hagen's face lit up and he asked if I were related to the Grondahls of Boscobel, Wisconsin. When I said that I was, he loudly called to everyone at the picnic that I was related to them and to make a place for me. With his arm around my shoulder, he took me around to various people and introduced me to the Lunds, the Jordahls, the Larsons, the Olsons, as well as the members of his own Hagen family. What I had so fortuitously stumbled into, Erik Hagen explained, was a gathering of the descendants of the early immigrants that had settled the little dying village that I had just found. I was amused by the fact that everyone spoke with such a thick, Scandinavian brogue, as if they had only recently arrived from the Old Country themselves.

Kent Grondahl admitted that for him the high point of the afternoon was meeting Kari Rogness, a beautiful, blue-eyed blonde who appeared to be about his own age. After only a few moments at her side, he found her completely enchanting. While other members of the gathering came from all over the United States for the annual reunion of settlers' families, he was delighted to discover that Kari was a local resident.

> The only aspect of that afternoon that was unpleasant was the constant intrusion of Svald. He cut

in several times when Kari was trying to teach me the polka, and he just seemed always to be hanging around within earshot. I finally asked Kari what the Incredible Hulk was to her, and she just giggled and said that Svald was kind of like her watchdog. A brother, a cousin, hopefully not a boyfriend, I wanted to know. Kari just laughed and said not to pay any attention to Svald. It was like someone asking you not to pay any attention to a huge grizzly bear that kept coming up to smell your pockets for food.

As would be expected of any red-blooded youth, Kent Grondahl asked to see Kari again. Although she had seemed so warm and friendly during the afternoon and had seen to it that he had received generous portions of the lavish smorgasbord, she now appeared cool and indifferent. Whenever he pressured her for her telephone number or address, she turned away and told him that it would not be wise to pursue a relationship.

Grondahl knew that it was time for him to get back to his studies. And all around him the families were packing up their things. Looking around in puzzlement, he asked where they had parked their cars. Erik Hagen explained that they had all left their vehicles in the village and had walked out to the picnic grounds. That was part of the annual ritual they observed.

I got back in my car and waved good-bye to Kari, who returned my wave with an expression of sorrow, which I took to be a sign of encouragement

133

that she already missed me and wanted to see me again. Directly behind her, like a faithful, towering mastiff, stood Svald, glaring at me as if I were vermin in his eyes.

Study was impossible. I spent half the night disturbing Jim, my roommate, as he tried to write a paper for English lit, regaling him with my descriptions of the wondrous Kari. My miserable performance on the econ test the next day was one of the deciding factors in changing my major to political science.

I found many listings under "Rogness" in the local telephone book, but none of them had a daughter named Kari. Determined to find her, I drove back to the small village and inquired of all the present residents about Kari Rogness. All of them agreed that Kari Rogness was a good Scandinavian name, but none of them gave me the slightest satisfaction as to her whereabouts. They were either lying, or Kari herself had lied to me about her true name and residency.

Persistent to the bitter end, on my next excursion to the locale, I drove down the long lanes of every farm within a radius of fifteen or twenty miles, seeking somehow to find the beautiful Kari.

One night, several weeks later, Kent Grondahl was seated at the counter in an all-night diner when he looked up to make sudden eye contact in the large counter mirror with Erik Hagen, who was sitting in a booth directly behind him with the brutish Svald. Grondahl was startled to see them there, for he was certain there had been no one else in the diner but one other man seated at the other end of the counter. Erik beckoned for him to join them.

Erik Hagen no longer spoke in his thick, Scandinavian brogue. In fact, I really couldn't identify the peculiar manner in which he now accented his words. I had no trouble understanding his message, however. He said that he and his friends had really liked me (though I questioned Svald's affection), but I should stop trying to find Kari. As she had told me honestly, a relationship with her was out of the question.

When I asked about his statement at the picnic that I was related to him, Erik smiled and said that was true. "We are related, but not in the way that you probably understand it," he tried to explain. "We are related to you as companions, as friends. There are those among us, like Svald here, who have some resentment toward your kind because truly, we were here first, and sometimes we feel supplanted by you and your kind. But hear me now, young Grondahl, because we feel a true affection for you, we are telling you to give up your search for Kari. What you hope for, can never be."

The waitress yelled that my hamburger was ready, and when I turned away from the counter, Erik and Svald were already out the door. I followed them into the street because I had so many questions that I wanted answered, but they were now nowhere to be seen.

Three years later, when he was visiting a friend in New York, Kent was certain that he saw Kari Rogness and Erik Hagen walking on the street in Times Square as he rode in a cab.

Like an idiot, I rolled down the window and shouted their names. I know they saw me and heard me, for they looked directly at me, then turned quickly away and stepped into the lobby of a movie theater. I cannot help wondering how many "Eriks," "Karis," and all of our other "relatives" walk among us, skillfully blending in with the crowd, carefully shielding their true identities and their true purpose from us.

Many years ago, in his book *Adventures with Phantoms*, British author Thurston Hopkins wondered similarly about the mysterious entities that he had encountered while walking the streets of London. Hopkins thought these beings "not fully quick, nor fully dead." In his opinion, these entities mimic us and pretend to be as we are, but they are not of us.

They are creatures who have strayed away from some unknown region of haunted woods and perilous wilds. They dress like us; pretend that they belong to mankind and profess to keep our laws and code of morals. But in their presence we are always aware that they are phantoms and that all their ideas and actions are out of key with the general pitch and tone of normal life.

Bizarre Encounters with Spirit Mimics on the Highways

Over the thirty-two years that various versions of the Steiger questionnaire have been distributed, many of those individuals who have filed lengthy reports describing their experiences with the unknown have testified to encountering what appear to be Spirit Mimics, or perhaps actual human entities somehow out of sync with time and space, on the highways.

Mary of Portland, Oregon, writes to say that she was driving east out of Bend on the Bend-Burns Highway early one morning. "The road is raised up somewhat—banked—from the desert and it is a long, easy slope down from Horse Ridge. I wasn't going very fast, just enjoying the drive, when I came up on a black sedan moving slowly. I hit my passing gear and zoomed past. As I passed, I looked in to see if there was anyone I knew in the sedan. There was just an older man and woman who looked back at me."

But when Mary glanced in her rearview mirror, just as soon as she had passed the black sedan, there was no car behind her. "The highway behind me was empty."

Mary had a frightening thought that the older couple had somehow gone over the bank, which, at that point, was several feet high. "I came to a quick stop at the edge of the road and got out. I went to the back of my car and looked and looked, but I couldn't see the black sedan anywhere. There were no access roads around or any other cars around. Besides, the car was only out of my sight for a couple of seconds."

As Mary stood there looking around for some sign of the mysterious black sedan with the older couple inside, "a light breeze sprang up and blew across me—and I can tell you that the hairs on the back of my neck and my arms stood up. I jumped in my little car, locked all four doors, and got out of there. I was both frightened and puzzled. I guess I still am. I still get that creepy hair-rising-on-back-of-neck-and-arms feeling whenever I recall the car that disappeared and the breeze that sprang up out of nowhere."

Early on a Sunday evening in 1991, Max was driving with his family outside of Albany, New York, when he became impatient with the way an old car, which he guessed to be a 1941 Chevrolet sedan, was slowing traffic. Max figured that the car was going to or coming from some antique auto show or rally and he wanted to be tolerant, but they were returning from a family outing at Lake George and he wanted to get home to do some paperwork.

"I had to be at work early the next morning with my presentation ready to go, and I had some factors that I needed to sharpen," Max said. "As I approached nearer to the Chevy, I was surprised that it didn't have those special license plates that owners of those old cars are supposed to display. I hated to be a jerk, but I really leaned on my horn, something I usually don't do when following a slow-moving vehicle."

Max recalled that he could see the driver of the

Chevy turn around and look at him with what appeared to be shock. "I expected an angry, hostile look, and maybe an obscene gesture or two, but this guy looked as if I had genuinely startled him. As if he had somehow imagined himself to be driving all alone on the highway."

Then, before the startled, incredulous eyes of Max, his wife, and their three children, the old Chevrolet sedan in front of them began to fade away. "It was as if it were some old photograph dissolving bit by bit before us, just fading away until there was nothing left to prove that it had ever been there. The antique Chevy and its driver had completely disappeared in about thirty seconds."

In the early summer of 1987, Sam and Clara were traveling to Amarillo, Texas, on a business trip. Shortly after midnight, they decided to stop to eat at a quaint, rustic-style restaurant that neither of them had ever noticed on previous trips to the region. They remember that the food was prepared in an excellent down-home style, and the waitress, the cook, and the other customers were so friendly in a sincere manner that Sam and Clara truly meant their promise that they would stop back again.

"And we tried to do exactly that on our return drive," Sam said, "but that great little down-home restaurant was nowhere to be seen. We even looped back a couple of times, thinking we might somehow have driven on by. We even got into an argument, each of us insisting that we remembered exactly where it was. We just couldn't find it, and since the hour was getting very late, we drove on."

Because their business required a number of return visits to Amarillo, Sam and Clara traveled that route on three consecutive weekends, each time keeping a watch for the restaurant with the wonderful cooking, but it seemed as though it had simply vanished.

"Since then, we have driven that route a dozen or more times," Sam said, "but we never again found that friendly little restaurant."

Indeed, Sam and Clara may have been extremely fortunate. What if the "friendly little restaurant" appeared and disappeared every few years? They could truly have been lost in time and space for decades.

In the next chapter we shall discover that the spirits of animals also have their place in Shadow World. While certain religionists may debate the reality of souls for God's "lesser creatures," for those who have experienced a joyful reunion with a beloved pet that has returned from the Other Side, such arguments have no merit.

CHAPTER SEVEN

Animal Spirits that Defied Death

Our late friend Bryce Bond was one of the world's most respected explorers of the unknown, a published author, and the host of "Dimensions in Parapsychology," for many years a popular television program in the New York metropolitan area. Besides sharing an interest in investigating the unexplained, Bryce shared our love of animals—and before he made his own transition to the Other Side, he received astounding proof that our pets also survive the grave.

During his marriage of twenty-three years, Bryce and his wife purchased a French poodle that they named Pepe. The dog was a black male with a zest for life and for exploration. He was small in size, but large in love. Both Bryce and his wife loved Pepe very much, and he became the child that they had never had. They shared with him a happy balance of love, and Pepe returned that energy of tenderness and affection to them.

Bryce admitted that although his marriage had its joys and happiness, it also had a good many fights and bickerings.

"Pepe became the pacifier," he said. "He appeared to love both of us equally, and he did not like our fighting. When we were quarreling, he would come to both of us and give us a little loving, as if to say, 'Stop it! Enough!'"

However, as the years went on, Bryce was sorry to say, the fighting between his wife and him increased.

"Sadly, little Pepe took on the frustrations, the anger, the pain that we were expressing toward each other," Bryce said. "He absorbed the emotional disharmony until it manifested in his body as cancer. On one level, we can probably say that Pepe took on the cancer that was meant for my wife or myself. Remember, he loved us equally, so he allowed our anger to become manifest in his tiny body."

As the cancer became increasingly painful for Pepe, the Bonds sought professional help for him. "But all the veterinarians said the same thing. Pepe was too far gone. Nothing could be done but to put him to sleep."

When Bryce could not restrain himself from asking yet another expert in animal treatment if there wasn't something that could be done to help Pepe, the doctor answered rather sharply, "Nothing! In fact, you should have done this months ago. This poor creature has been in so much pain, and he has suffered far too long."

Bryce indicated that the doctor should proceed, and the veterinarian softened his attitude and compassionately explained that Pepe would not feel anything but a very gentle drowsiness before he slipped into the final sleep.

"I took Pepe's head in my hands and held him very close to me," Bryce said. "I was half crying, half telling him that it was all right. I was with him. He licked my fingers. I kissed him on the top of his head and whispered from my heart, 'I love you. Good-bye, my friend.'"

The doctor administered the lethal injection, and Pepe relaxed and fell asleep. There were no twitching muscles. Pepe had peacefully gone home.

Bryce and his wife placed their dear Pepe's body in a wooden box and began the seven-hour drive to her home in Virginia. "We had agreed to bury Pepe there on my wife's family peanut farm. He had loved it there, because he could run free without any big city restrictions."

The next day the Bonds covered Pepe with his favorite blanket and placed some of his favorite toys with him in the wooden box. Then they closed the lid for the last time, nailed it shut, buried the box, and covered the area with pine branches.

"The loss of anyone or anything connected to you by the bond of love is painful," Bryce said. "But I knew that as long as I had memory, I would always be connected to Pepe. He was the child I never had, and he was also a teacher to me."

* * *

Several months after Pepe had died, Bryce and his wife decided to divorce. At the same time, Bryce also decided to end his career in radio broadcasting. He knew that he was at a transition point in his life and that he was given an opportunity to be of greater service to humankind as a healer.

Three years after Pepe's death, Bryce was lying in bed ready for sleep. "My physical body was just about to drift into the sleep state when I felt something jump up on the bed and land at my feet. At first I thought it was part of my dream cycle, but the *something* began to circle around, then settle on my feet with physical weight and body heat. My eyes were closed, so I kept them closed. I wanted to experience the experience!"

In Bryce Bond's consciousness, he *knew* that it was Pepe come to pay a visit, for the dog had always joined him in bed in just such a manner. "Thank you, God!" he rejoiced in his heart.

Pepe then got up and slowly walked the length of Bryce's body until he reached his head. Bryce was able to feel a smallish body depressing the mattress with actual physical weight as it moved upward.

"Then Pepe brushed against my face about seven times," he said. "I kept my eyes tightly shut. I was overjoyed. I wanted this to happen. I feared that if I opened my eyes this wonderful experience would cease."

Bryce reached out in the darkness, his eyes still closed.

"I felt his tail with one hand, his cool, wet nose with the other," he said. "Next I moved my hand to his stomach, and as I stroked the area, I felt the small hernia that he had—and I felt him breathe. His stomach was soft and warm to the touch. I could smell the scent of him without any mistake. It was my Pepe!

"In spite of my joy, I did not open my eyes throughout the entire experience, which lasted for about ten minutes. Then, at last, Pepe was gone. I once again gave thanks to God for the experience."

After the visitation, Bryce remembered that he fell into a deep and very peaceful sleep. When he awakened the next morning and replayed the events of the previous evening in his mind, he noticed that there were clumps of black hair wedged under each of his fingernails. *Poodle hair.*

"I trembled with excitement over the additional proof that Pepe had given me to bring peace to my heart and to demonstrate that he was all right," Bryce said. "Later, I had the hairs analyzed by a veterinarian and a forensic chemist. It was, indeed, poodle hair. And as any poodle owner knows, poodles don't shed. Pepe had provided me with physical proof that consciousness survives. Such events are gifts from God!"

Since he relayed that marvelous story of a loving dog's return to provide proof of the afterlife, our good friend Bryce Bond has made his own transition into the world beyond death. Somewhere in that beautiful dimension that we call Heaven, I know that he and Pepe are walking new trails of discovery.

Nearly Half of All Pet Owners Believe They Will Be Reunited with Their Pets in the Afterlife

In 1991, the *National Enquirer* published the results of a fascinating poll that they had taken in five major U.S. cities—Los Angeles, New York, Dallas, Philadelphia, and Washington, D.C.—regarding the question of whether or not pet owners believed that their pets would join them in Heaven. Nearly half (49 percent) of the animal lovers queried were certain that they would spend eternity with their pets. Interestingly, more men (56 percent) than women (46 percent) expected to walk around Heaven with their pets strolling beside them.

If 49 percent of the pet owners surveyed believed that their pet possessed a soul and would accompany them to the Other Side, then we might assume that at least that same percentage of animal lovers would not be at all surprised if the spirit of their deceased pet returned to make contact with them or to bid them farewell.

Tom Muzila is a former Green Beret with a fifth-degree black belt in Shorokan karate who serves as a martial arts advisor for many motion pictures. Tom tells of the sad day when his beloved pit bull, Algonquin, died—and then came back to say good-bye.

"We had such a close bond, and I mourned him that night by lighting white candles and saying a prayer for him. Later that night, I was awakened by a familiar

scratching at my bedroom door. I knew it was Algonquin. His presence was strong. I drifted back into a
light sleep, then I felt him jump on my bed. His loving
spirit stayed near me for seven days, then it left to return to the Oneness."

Beany Came to the Hospital for a Final Visit

When Margaret Manthey was sixteen, she was involved in a serious accident in her hometown in Iowa.
It had been a hot day in August, and she and her
friend Rose Ann were riding their bicycles to get an ice
cream soda at the corner drugstore with Margaret's
faithful beagle, Beany, in close pursuit. None of them
saw the car that roared past the stop sign after making
an incomplete stop. Later, witnesses would say that
the driver seemed in an alcoholic daze or some kind of
altered state of consciousness as he accelerated directly
toward the teenagers and the beagle.

"All that I know," Margaret said, "was that something hard had hit my side, and I was flying through
the air. It seemed to take forever before I hit the side-
walk and rolled over on my back. I think I was
knocked out for a while, and the next thing I remember was Rose Ann kneeling beside me, crying, holding
my hand. Faces of men and women bobbed up and
down above me, and I heard a lady say that she had
called the police and an ambulance. I knew that I must

be saying something, but my voice sounded so far away that I couldn't hear what I was saying."

Margaret's time in the emergency room is equally distorted in her memory. Although it felt to her as if she had broken every bone in her body and skinned every square inch of flesh, she heard the doctor talking about a mild concussion and order two nurses to clean up all the scratches. She also understood that she was to spend the next two nights in the hospital for observation.

Later, when she lay back against the pillows in her hospital bed, she began to cry.

"I had been staying with Rose Ann because my parents were out of town for a few days," Margaret said. "I wasn't such a grownup that I didn't want my mom and dad there with me. And Beany! How I wished that my best friend in the whole world was with me to lick my face and be with me in these strange surroundings."

Margaret explained that Beany had slept on her bed every night since she was ten. The energetic beagle had been her faithful companion, never scolding her or contradicting her. He had listened to all of her complaints about boyfriends, teachers, and the "terribly unfair" rules of her parents. And when she told Beany a secret, she could be certain that the beagle's lips were sealed.

During that first night in the hospital, Margaret was awakened by something pushing up against her feet. She sat up as far as her throbbing head would permit, and she was startled to see Beany sleeping near her feet. Her loyal friend had found some way to get into the hospital unnoticed. Margaret was so happy to see him, but she was also concerned about what would happen if any of the nurses discovered a dog in her room.

Beany snuggled up to her and licked her face. "After I hugged him for a few minutes, I told him that he had better go home before someone caught him in the hospital," Margaret said. "Beany whined and moved even closer to my chest. I remember wincing at the pain from my bruised ribs."

Just then a nurse entered her room with a flashlight, and Beany jumped down and ran to a shadowy corner.

"I decided to explain in my best adult manner that my dog had missed me so much and had been so concerned for me that he had somehow managed to get into the hospital," Margaret said. "I asked her not to be angry, and perhaps, I suggested, some kind person might take Beany home to Rose Ann's."

The nurse moved the flashlight beam all around the room. She smiled and told Margaret that she had been dreaming. There was no dog in the room. She poured Margaret a fresh glass of water and said that she would return with something to help her sleep better.

"I concluded that tricky old Beany had managed to beat it out of there without the nurse seeing him," Margaret said. "I glanced at the big round wall clock and saw that it was nearly four-thirty a.m. I took the pill the nurse gave me, and I thought maybe by the time that I woke up, Mom and Dad would be there."

When her parents arrived later that morning, the

first thing Margaret wanted after all their hugs and kisses was to know if Beany had got home all right. She explained how the beagle had sneaked into the hospital in the middle of the night, so she hoped that he made it home safely.

"The look that passed between my parents hurt more than the concussion," Margaret said, concluding her story. "Dad explained that they had arrived back home from their trip about three-thirty a.m. They had found a trail of blood that led to the back porch, one of Beany's favorite hiding places. It was immediately apparent to them that Beany had been hit by the car at the same time that I had. In his pain and confusion, he had run back home. My parents sat up with him, trying their best to comfort him. Beany had died about four a.m. I will always cherish the memory of his final visit to me in the hospital—a visit that my dear, faithful Beany made from doggy heaven."

Sluggo Came to Say Good-bye

Karen B. of San Diego told of her strange experience on October 14, 1987, when she heard the unmistakable yowling of her big tabby, Juniper.

"I was astonished to see the old guy standing at my bedroom door, looking at something in the hallway that was obviously terrifying him," Karen said. "His mouth was wide open, hissing and spitting. His ears were drawn back close to his head. Naturally, I was becoming pretty scared myself, wondering just what in heck was in my hallway that was so frightening."

Reluctantly, Karen went to investigate, carrying clutched in her right hand the baseball bat that her father insisted she keep handy under her bed. She broke into nervous laughter when she saw that the only thing in the hallway was her little black-and-white terrier, Sluggo.

She scolded Juniper for scaring the bejabbers out of both of them. "What's wrong with you, you silly cat? Is this some kind of weird cat game, pretending you're afraid of your buddy Sluggo?"

Karen remembered that Sluggo just stood there, cocking his head from side to side. "He almost looked as though his feelings had been hurt by Juniper behaving that way toward him. I had had Sluggo for six years and Juniper for four, and the two animals had always got along together just fine."

The doorbell rang, and Karen went to answer it, calling over her shoulder to Sluggo, "Don't take it personally, buddy. Juniper is just being weird. Maybe he got into some catnip or something." She opened the door to admit her next-door neighbor, Hank Swanson, who carried the limp body of a small black-and-white terrier in his arms.

"I'm so sorry, Karen," he told her. "This van came roaring down the street and hit Sluggo. Didn't even stop. I saw it all happen. Sluggo died right away, though. Thank God, he didn't suffer."

Karen said that she had to struggle with reality for several moments before she could speak. It *couldn't* be Sluggo that Hank was holding. Sluggo was in the hallway where Juniper was still hissing at him as if he were seeing . . . a *ghost*!

She managed to mumble her thanks to Hank Swanson for his kindness and concern, then she took the crumpled, lifeless body of her faithful dog in her arms and wept softly. It was Sluggo. She recognized his collar, his dog tag, his familiar rumpled fur.

Juniper was still frozen in a posture of fear, but there was no longer any image of Sluggo in the hallway.

"When I gently lay Sluggo's body down in his doggy bed, Juniper suddenly broke free from the rigid trauma that had held him fast, and he dashed behind the dresser where he remained for the rest of the evening," Karen said. "It took several days before he was able to enter the hallway without trembling, then running as fast as he could to the kitchen. Sluggo had come to bid us good-bye, but he had nearly scared the life out of Juniper in the process."

Bachelor Bouley's Hellhounds

While it would seem that the great majority of accounts of animal spirits tell of benign and loving entities that returned to their owners for a final visit or a reassurance that life goes on beyond physical death, there are those tales that speak of more hostile and frightening animal beings that come charging out of Shadow World. Such an account was submitted for my files on the paranormal by Russell Madsen of Missouri.

"Not far from where I grew up there's an old

haunted, burned-out farm down a long lane that's called Bachelor Bouley's Hellhole," Madsen said in his report.

"There are half a dozen stories about Bachelor Bouley and any and all of them might be true. Some say he was a bootlegger and his still blew up and burned down his barn and his house, where he lived with about a dozen 'coon hounds. Others say that Bouley was some kind of black magic man and when the devil came one night to collect Bouley's soul, his flaming footprints caught old Bouley's house on fire. Still others insist that some angry, self-righteous folk who judged Bouley an old reprobate burned the house to the ground with him and all his howling hounds inside, sizzling and frying to death with their master."

Madsen said that there were two consistent elements in the legends about Bouley: that he was a cranky old recluse whose only companions were a dozen or more hunting dogs that lived, ate, and slept with him in his ramshackle farm house; and that the angry spirits of those hounds that were burned alive with their master still protected the place.

According to Madsen,

Over the years it had become a rite of passage for teenage boys to drive out to Bachelor Bouley's Hellhole and tempt the ghost hounds to chase them. Dozens of people over the years swore that there was really something hellish out there on the place, and there were all kinds of testimonials about ripped clothes, clawed fenders, and scratched faces that were attributed to Bouley's hellhounds.

Madsen said that he had become a believer at a very young age. "The thing was, still bearing fruit on Bouley's burned-out farm was an orchard with the best-tasting apples in the Western world. The rule was, you just didn't go there after sundown."

When Madsen was around ten, he and his eight-year-old sister Cathy had walked across the fields to Bouley's orchard from their uncle's place where they had been staying while their parents were visiting relatives in St. Louis.

"It had taken us a little longer than we had estimated," Madsen said, "and the sun was just setting when we heard something moving toward us in the tall grass. Cathy looked at me and whispered, 'It's Bouley's hounds,' and we tore out of there as fast as we could, forgetting all about the pile of apples we had collected.

"We were nearly to the lane, which according to the legend was a kind of sacred borderline, when something sent both of us sprawling into the rough gravel. We could hear panting and growling all around us.

"I got up and started kicking at something holding on to my trouser leg, and Cathy was swinging her little arms like a windmill. Finally we got to the lane, and the hellhounds stopped chasing us and let us go."

When they returned to their uncle's place, they were both scratched and bleeding, and their clothes were ripped and torn in several places.

"Uncle Bob thought I had been rough-housing with Cathy, and he was about to get a switch for my bottom," Madsen remembered, "but Cathy swore that I hadn't pushed her or anything. 'Uncle Bob,' she said, her eyes still wide with fear, 'it was the hellhounds sure as I'm born.'

"Because just once I told a fib to Uncle Bob about breaking some eggs in the henhouse, he never believed a thing I told him," Madsen said. "Cathy, though, was the apple of his eye. If she told him that it was snowing purple flakes, he wouldn't even look outside to check out her story. Aunt Doris shuddered and told us never to go anywhere near the Bouley place ever again."

Russell Madsen said that he heeded his aunt's advice until it was time that he test his mettle against the hellhounds with his friends in his high school's peculiar rite of passage.

"When I was sixteen, my buddies and I heard that a bunch of senior football players had driven out to Bachelor Bouley's and gotten the devil scared out of them," Madsen continued with his account. "They said they heard the hounds baying and howling and jumping around their car. The toughest guy among them got out of the car and swore that something ripped the sleeve of his letter jacket. The others pulled him back in and they layed rubber getting out of there."

Madsen's friends Don, Todd, and Joe picked him up that night so that they could go see for themselves and test their manhood against Bouley's hellhounds.

"I tried to tell the guys that the stories about the ghost hounds were no bull," Madsen said. "I told them again, for the two-thousandth time, about what happened to Cathy and me in the orchard six years ago. Of course, they all snickered and said that we were just little kids then. Probably scared ourselves over a big squirrel chasing us."

Don had managed to get his father's new station wagon with the story that the gang was going to a drive-in movie. "Don considered himself a real intellectual," Madsen said. "He was always talking about scientific proof and the advances of modern science and how he was going to be a research chemist someday. I think the only reason he wanted to go to Bachelor Bouley's was to debunk the whole idea of ghost dogs and have a good laugh at the expense of the senior football guys who had gotten the crap scared out of them."

Sooner than it seemed possible, Don was heading the station wagon down the long lane to the burned-out old farmstead.

"I wonder why no one has ever built a new farmhouse on the place," Joe wondered out loud.

"Because of the damned hellhounds!" Todd answered sharply. Madsen says the way Todd's eyes were moving from side to side as they drove down the lane, it seemed obvious that he would really rather be at the drive-in.

"Don pulled up next to the charred ruins of the house and shut off the headlights," Madsen said. "He told us that he wanted to be able to see if the ghost dogs' eyes really glowed in the dark."

And then, according to Madsen,

All around the car we could hear the sounds of things moving, sounding very much like a milling pack of very large dogs. Within moments we could hear—and feel—some very solid *things* bumping themselves up against the sides, hood, and rear of the station wagon. Joe wanted to get the hell out of there. Todd just sat there shivering. I pleaded with Don not to get out to investigate as he claimed he was going to do before we left town.

And then the howling started. A high-pitched, mournful howling that I know I shall remember for the rest of my life. Todd clamped his hands over his ears and began to cry. Joe, sitting in the front seat beside Don, punched him in the shoulder and shouted at him to burn rubber and get us the hell out of there. Don seemed paralyzed, as if he were somehow mesmerized by the terrible frequency of the spirit dogs' ear-piercing howls. At last, he managed to shake himself free of the fear or the fascination that had held him immobile, and he tore out of the place as if we were truly escaping from the outer rim of hell.

The next day was a Saturday, and when I went over to Don's house to talk over the incredible events of the night before, he was catching hell from his father. The new station wagon was covered with dozens of scratches, scratches like the paws of very large dogs would make, and Don's father wanted to know what kind of drive-in movie could produce effects like those.

Russell Madsen concluded his story by stating that none of his friends ever went out to Bachelor Bouley's Hellhole during the rest of their years in high school. "But I hear that teenage boys still have to drive out to Bouley's," he said. "Like I said, it's like some kind of rite of passage for boys in that region."

The Terrible Cat Creature at the Top of the Stairs

John Pendragon, the late British clairvoyant and seer, told me the following eerie account of a demonic ghost cat while we were collaborating on his biography, *Pendragon—A Clairvoyant's Power of Prophecy* (New York: Award Books; London: Tandem Books, 1968).

It was a very distressed Howard Leland who came to Pendragon on an October afternoon in 1943. Perhaps more than anything else, the man wished to receive validation of his supernatural experience and be told that he was not going crazy.

Leland began his account by explaining that he was a volunteer with the A.R.P. (Air Raid Precautions) and that a couple of nights previously, during a raid of Nazi bombers over South London, he had taken shelter in a deserted house.

"I sat on the bottom step of the old staircase," he said, "and after a few minutes, I had the uncomfortable feeling that something was watching me from the top of the stairs.

"I clicked on my torch and flashed the beam upwards. I was scared half out of my wits to see a blackish-brown, hairy creature that looked very much like an extremely large tabby cat squatting on the top stair—and I swear to the Almighty that the bloody thing had horns sticking out of its head!"

Leland paused to measure a distance from his forehead to indicate the approximate length of the protuberances.

"And the terrible thing had long, sharp-looking claws, I mean to tell you," he continued. "The wretched beast and I stared at each other for fully half a minute—and I tell you, I shall never forget the evil that shone in those eyes. I'm not ashamed to admit that I was too scared to either advance or retreat."

Fortunately, Leland said, it was at that point that two of his buddies with the A.R.P. entered through the open front door of the old house, and the hellish cat—or whatever it was—leaped from its squatting position and seemed to run down the hall.

Leland explained to them as best he could what he had seen; and strangely enough, they did not laugh at him or give him a bad time about drinking on his watch.

"One of my mates told me that the hideous creature had been seen off and on in the neighborhood for years," Leland told Pendragon. "The old place had for a time been turned into a boarding house, and numerous previous residents had witnessed the thing. Always, it seems, the monstrous cat creature was seen sitting at the top of the stairs, in the very same spot that I had seen him."

Pendragon asked him if the men had gone upstairs to look for any physical signs to corroborate the cat's actual existence.

Leland nodded. He had felt more courageous in the company of his fellow A.R.P. volunteers, and they had walked upstairs to investigate. "We found not a thing," he said, shaking his head.

Then Leland narrowed his eyes and wagged a forefinger for emphasis. "But I *did* see that hideous creature on the stairs, and no one can convince me otherwise! I am not subject to hallucinations, and I most certainly had not taken a drink while I was on duty that night."

Pendragon laughed softly. "There's no need to convince me. I am most happy to take your word for your encounter. What interests me is *why* the creature was there. Please give me the address of the building."

Pendragon wrote down the address that Leland supplied, and he concentrated on it for several moments. No impressions came.

He rose from his desk and stood before a large scale map of London that he had tacked to the wall months before while he was doing research on a series of hauntings in a particular section of the city. Looking closely at the map, he located the building in question— just a tiny dot amidst the thousands of dwellings in South London.

But the moment Pendragon placed his forefinger on the minuscule dot, he suddenly "saw" the darkened stairway that was the lair of the hideous horned cat creature.

In Pendragon's paranormal vision, something moved from the shadows. Not a creature, but a man. A despondent man who had sought to better his position in life by engaging in the practice of seeking to summon spirits from the Dark Side, a truly smarmy endeavor that had included the ritual sacrifice of dozens of cats on his perverse satanic altar.

Pendragon's highly developed psychic abilities permitted him to view a most extraordinary re-creation of a past event. Swirling about the devil worshipper as he walked toward the top of the stairs were the spirit forms of many cats whose hearts had been ripped from their bodies by his cruel sacramental dagger. Pendragon reeled in a moment of vertigo as he felt the hatred of dozens of feline psyches focused on their murderer.

Then the clairvoyant noticed that the man carried with him a rope in which he had fashioned a noose. There was a brilliant flurry of macabre images, and Pendragon suddenly felt a violent constriction of his throat. Coughing spasmodically, he removed his forefinger from the map and reached for the cup of tea on his desk.

"If you will make inquiries," Pendragon told Leland after he had allowed the soothing tea to calm him, "I am certain that you will find that a previous owner of the house committed suicide by hanging himself from the banister at the top of the stairs."

"And the awful cat creature?" Leland wanted to know.

Pendragon nodded. "Yes, it is there. It is quite likely an elemental spirit that has assumed the general form of the dozens of cats that this disturbed fellow sacrificed on his satanic altar."

"An elemental?" Leland echoed. "And what's all this about satanic rites?"

"The man hanged himself in utmost despondency when his attempts to better himself through the black arts and animal sacrifice failed," the psychic explained. "Elementals are rather low-level spirit entities that are prone to frequent places where a tragedy—generally suicide or murder—has occurred. They are also sometimes associated with places where black magic rites have been performed. They can become a kind of personification of evil."

Pendragon ended his account by stating that Howard Leland returned to his office before a week had passed to provide an interesting follow up of the clairvoyant's impressions.

"I don't know how you managed to peg it," Leland said, "but I learned from longtime residents in the neighborhood that a previous resident did, indeed, hang himself from a banister.

"Before the man killed himself," Leland continued, "folks said that they had been bothered in the middle of the night by the sounds of cats yowling and screaming coming from the house. And it was shortly after the man hanged himself that people started seeing that terrible horned cat thing at the top of the stairs.

"I guess it's like the old Bard of Avon said it, there really are more things between heaven and earth than can be dreamt of in anyone's philosophy," Leland concluded.

Did the Ghost Dog Kill the Baby?

In May 1955, on the first weekend that the Fred Perry family spent in their new home in Birmingham, England, they were awakened by the sound of a slamming door.

Perry got out of bed to investigate, puzzled because he knew that he had carefully locked all the doors before retiring that evening.

As he stood in the kitchen, he heard a scraping sound like the noise a scrambling animal might make. It was as if an invisible dog were somehow scampering around him. After a few moments of such eerie, unexplained sounds, the house was silent and Perry returned to bed.

As time passed, the Perrys were visited nightly by an array of strange sounds. The greatest concentration of frightening noises occurred around midnight—and no matter how the doors had been secured, they banged to and fro, as if they possessed a will of their own. Eerie whispers of half-words and nearly understandable phrases echoed and swirled in the air around them.

Once, while cleaning the bedroom, Mrs. Perry experienced an awful sensation that felt like icy, unseen fingers running over her body. And the infernal sounds of the paws of that invisible dog seemed to follow them all over the house.

Fred and his wife had come to acknowledge that such manifestations could have no natural explanations, and they lay awake nights, listening and wondering. Their dream house had begun transforming itself into a nightmare, and they prayed that their two small sons and their baby boy would not be negatively affected by the bizarre occurrences.

Even though a sense of evil had clearly presented itself to the Perrys, they resolved to do their best not to give in to it. Both of them were certain that an expressed fear of the unseen entities would only give the dark energies greater power over them. They reasoned that only those people who feared supernatural forces could be harmed by them.

Then, one hot morning in June, the family awakened to the horror that their baby son had suffocated during the night. The Perrys' sorrow and sense of despair were only deepened by the fact that their baby had been in the best of health. When their family doctor examined the infant, he stated that he could find no mark of violence anywhere on his body or any discernible medical reason why he should have died so suddenly.

Shortly after the child's burial, the younger of their sons startled them by asking if his baby brother had gone away with the little dog.

The Perrys felt a shiver run through them. They knew for a certainty that no *physical* dog had ever entered their home. There were only those ghostly sounds of the unseen creatures scampering through the house.

"When did you see the little dog?" Perry asked the boy.

The child looked up at his father as if he were joking with him. "I used to see him nearly every day, and especially at night," he answered with a small giggle. "His little paws make so much noise on the wood floors. Surely, you must have seen him running through our house, up and down the stairs, everywhere. But he seems to have gone away."

Summoning her emotional reserve, Mrs. Perry asked her son when he had last seen the little dog.

"On the night the baby left us," he replied. "The little dog was sitting on the baby's face."

His wife became hysterical and Fred could not calm her. The thought that her child had died as a result of supernatural suffocation horrified her.

In an effort to exorcise the negative entities in the house, they summoned a priest, but the religious ritual performed by the clergyman did nothing to quiet the hostile spirits. The nocturnal bumping and banging continued unabated, and the scratching and scampering of the ghost dog had definitely returned.

Then, on one of the first days in July, Fred Perry became aware of foreboding whispers of greater volume than he had ever experienced in the house. The essence of evil became so strong that he feared for his wife and his two sons.

He rushed to the stairs where a frightening scene awaited him. His wife stood on the landing, transfixed with terror. Her limbs had stiffened and her hands were frozen to her sides. The veins on her neck had swollen. Her eyes bulged with terror, and her mouth gaped open in a silent scream. She looked as if some giant, monstrous hand had caught her and was squeezing the very life out of her.

When Fred ran up the stairs to help her, he encountered an invisible force that would not allow him to pass. It seemed to shroud him as if it were a giant spider's web.

At last, with a powerful lunge, he was able to break through the unseen wall of evil, and at that same instant, his wife's screams filled the house.

Without bothering to pack, the Perrys took their children and left the house, resigning the place to the demonic dog and whatever monstrous thing it deemed its master.

Later, friends of the Perrys collected their belongings. They, too, heard the strange whispers, the weird thumpings, and the scratching and scampering of the invisible dog. Once they had finished packing, they agreed with the Perrys that no inducement could bring them back into the accursed house.

CHAPTER EIGHT

Nature Spirits: Devas or Devils?

One evening just after sunset as I was doing the evening chores on our farm in Iowa, I heard screams coming from the gravel road at the end of our lane.

There was still enough light for me to see three girls on bicycles and since I was seventeen at the time, I couldn't help entertaining the notion that maybe they were coming to visit me. But it was soon apparent, as I set down my pails of corn and oats for the livestock and gave full attention to the cyclists, that these girls were really afraid of something, for they were screaming bloody murder and peddling their bikes as fast as they could manage on the loose gravel.

Before I could get to my car and drive down to investigate whatever it might have been that had so frightened them, they were nearly out of sight.

Although we had a long lane, our community was

small enough for me to be pretty certain who the girls were, so the next time I went to town, I located one of them and asked her what had caused them to scream as if their very lives were in danger.

According to Sandy, the three friends had decided to go on a twilight bike ride in the country. Just as they passed our lane, a large ball of glowing greenish-white light rose up out of the ditch and began to bob about near them, as if checking out each one of them individually. They screamed and turned their bicycles around and headed back toward town, but the ball followed them for about a quarter of a mile before it turned around and left them.

I listened with polite interest to their spooky story, but I was certain that the three "townies" had been frightened by a cluster of lightning bugs that had risen up out of the ditch when they were disturbed by the girls' approach.

A couple of nights later as I was driving home in my 1948 maroon Ford coupe, I was startled to see a greenish-white glowing orb of light bobbing ahead of me right square in the middle of the road. It appeared to me to be about the size of a volley ball.

I didn't really have time to slam on the brakes to avoid hitting the thing, and I had only a few seconds to worry about whether or not it would explode if I struck it. The strange illuminated ball solved my dilemma by passing through the windshield, remaining a few moments right at chest-level directly in front of the steering wheel, then moving around me to pass out the rear window.

Although it had appeared to be a solid ball of some luminous substance, it had passed through my little Ford without doing either the automobile or itself any discernible damage.

And whether it just thought it was fun to startle me or if it was on some mysterious mission, the ball of light seemed to be waiting for me near the same clump of trees on the next two consecutive evenings.

After those three close encounters with the mysterious glowing globe, I didn't meet another one until several years later, while driving a lonely country road late at night. On that occasion, the light swerved away from my car and shot at great speed across an open field.

I have since studied will-o'-the-wisp–type phenomena and the electrical manifestations of ball lightning, but I really don't believe either theory applies to my encounter. What is obvious, however, is that they are an apparently universal experience.

Multiplying Green Balls of Light

In April 1998, Jeff Rense and I received the following email after one of our monthly ghost nights on his internationally heard "Sightings" radio show (and I must say that it is typical of dozens of letters that I receive each year).

A very strange thing happened to a friend and me one night about six years ago. I will never forget it, and I've been looking for an explanation ever since. We were in my car driving in Ohio when we encountered small green balls of light (there was one orange one) that flew all around us. Somehow they got inside the car, and they multiplied until the entire car was full of them. They had consistency, because when they would hit our arms and so forth, we could feel them. What were they? Spirits? Demons?

Believe me, mention these greenish balls of light on a radio talk show and the board lights up. Apparently thousands of people have had encounters with these mysterious globs of illumination.

A Mysterious Ball of Light Joined Her on Her Midnight Walk

Here is an eerie encounter with a mysterious globe of light that occurred in 1916 and was sent to me a few years ago by a Mrs. B.K.

In the spring of 1916 I was teaching a rural school near Wellsburg, Iowa, and boarding with a farm family. I was going with a young man in Wellsburg and very much in love, but he had been acting differently toward me lately, and I was worried. It was in late May, near the end of the school year, and on this particular night I was restless and couldn't sleep. So even though the hour was very late, around eleven, I got up, dressed, crept silently down the stairs, walked out the door, and went for a stroll.

It was a beautiful night, and a full moon was riding high in the sky. It had been an unusually warm spring, and it was almost like summer. I felt quite exhilarated and not at all afraid. All the farmers in the neighborhood were fast asleep, so there was little chance of meeting anyone on the little-traveled dirt road. I was enjoying my walk so much that I didn't notice how far I had gone, but it must have been two or three miles. As I realized that I must start back, the sky became overcast, covering the full moon and making the night darker and darker. My mood changed to an eerie sort of fear, and I kept walking faster and faster. Soon it was so dark that my fear almost became panic, for I could hardly see the road anymore.

At last I reached the crossroads near the farmhouse where I was staying. Then I suddenly turned my head and looked over my shoulder. There, just a few yards behind me, floating about three feet above the ground, was an orange-red ball or disc, following me at the same pace as I was walking. It glowed dully, but shed no light around it or on the ground. Almost as soon as I had seen it, it veered off to the side of the road, rose a bit, then sailed over the barbed-wire fence and disappeared in some shrubbery on the other side. It was with great relief that I got into the house and went back to bed.

I didn't tell my landlady about this for a day or two, because I did not want her to know about my midnight walk, but finally my curiosity got the better of me and I did tell her about what I had seen. She merely nodded and said, "We call them jack-o'-lanterns." From her response it was obvious that lots of other folks had seen them, but I sensed that she didn't care to talk more about the subject so I dropped it.

I'd heard of such things as the will-o'-the-wisp, but I always picture that as a rather formless white light, and this had been an orange-red globe. There were no swamps or marshes around, so it couldn't have been "swamp gas." My father once said something vague about "ball lightning," but if it had been that, it should have exploded. This strange ball of reddish light behaved as if it were intelligent, for it had been following me in a straight line—but as soon as it was discovered, it swerved aside and went into the bushes as if in hiding. And hadn't there been something unnatural about the sudden darkness? This experience remains among my unsolved mysteries.

Glowing Balls of Light and the Folklore of the Wee People

If such peculiar manifestations as these glowing balls of light should be intelligent, just what are they and what is their purpose? We have a folklore at least two thousand years old that links these mysterious globes of light with the nature spirits: the Devas, the elves, the fairies—whatever one chooses to label this companion species that occupies a considerable portion of Shadow World. Some say that the balls of light are themselves an intelligence that can manifest the physical appearance most compatible with the level of understanding of each individual witness.

The manipulation of glowing balls of light as a means of transportation may also be employed by angels and spirit guides. Indeed, the globes of light may be the form these benevolent beings assume before fully materializing in our dimension. Readers of my *Guardian Angels and Spirit Guides* (Plume/Penguin Inspiration, 1995; Signet Visions, 1998) will recall my description of witnessing a green globe of softly glowing light transform itself into a hooded, monklike figure.

In my over forty years as a student of the paranormal and as an investigator of the unexplained, I have now met many very sensible and serious-minded men and women who have claimed to have experienced an interaction with this mysterious companion species of intelligences. In most cases, especially if their encounters occurred when they were children, the contact seemed to be of a positive nature.

Meeting a Gnome Whose Job Is Energizing Plant Life

B.H. from Milwaukee writes that one day as she was relaxing in a lovely forest, admiring the beauty of nature's handiwork, she heard a small voice calling out, "Hello!"

As I looked down to where the voice echoed from, I saw a little gnome sitting on the trunk of a tree. I said, "Hello, to you, my little friend. What is your name?" He said I could call him "Pumpkin." He appeared less than two feet tall, but then, suddenly, he grew much larger for a moment, then shrunk back down. "I did that with the expansion and contraction of my breathing," he told me. "I knew you would like to see it."

Pumpkin explained that he worked with the vegetable kingdom, the plants and the shrubs. He and his kind energized the etheric bodies of the plant kingdom, so that all life can be maintained and strengthened. He stood up as though he heard someone call, then said to me, "I must go now." He smiled at me, then disappeared.

After my encounter with this wee, loving, happy person, I am more deeply in awe of God's Kingdoms and his Creations on our beautiful Earth.

Wee Friends and Advisors from Another Dimension

When I was conducting a research concerning the "wee people," I asked a friend of mine in a letter if she had ever seen nature spirits or entities, those beings commonly referred to as elves and fairies, she said that she was surprised to receive my letter.

"For a moment I wondered if somehow you had entered into this other dimension and had somehow traveled through space with these beings in disguise," she began her answer. "Somehow you have found out about my secret, and now I can admit that it is true."

My friend said that she had never before told anyone about her "wee people" experiences, but she now told me that she had interacted with these beings since her childhood.

> I think they come from another dimension. I may be sitting just kind of staring at the floor, and suddenly the specks on the floor will seem to move about and form a picture of one of these beings, and then there he is beside me. Sometimes there will be two, three, or more of these wonderful characters manifesting before me. A smile always crosses my lips because these beings are my friends. They've been with me for many years, since my early childhood. I know they are real, yet this is the first time that I have described them to anyone. Most people just wouldn't understand. And there are so many questions that I can't answer or explain.
>
> I don't know how or why it happens. It doesn't happen as often when I am depressed as when I am happy. I don't feel it is a psychic thing, like being in a trance or somehow willing the beings to appear. I suppose the manifestations of these beings make me wonder what is really real. Perhaps these unexplained things are more alive and perhaps more real than the so-called natural world around me.
>
> Sometimes these little beings talk to me, but their voices seem to come from inside my head. It's more often like a thought than a sound. Besides relaxing me and entertaining me, these entities help me in many ways. For instance, several days ago I was sitting quietly watching these little people as they danced for me. Suddenly one of them said, "Why are you so sad today?" Another one spoke up and said, "Instead of worrying about your problems,

why don't you help somebody?" As he danced away, he spoke again, "Remember, you can't help someone else without helping yourself, too." With that final comment, they all vanished.

I didn't completely understand the message, but it seemed nice, so I began to wonder who I could help. Later that day, I did have an opportunity to help someone; and while I didn't expect it to turn out the way it did, the immediate results opened a door that brought more help to me than anything else had done for a long time. I am always grateful to the Little People for their good advice.

Meeting the Nature Spirits of Sedona

There are those who will say that there are certain places on Earth where one can more readily contact such intelligent energies. Charmaine Yarune Boericke moved from Los Angeles to Sedona, Arizona, a few years ago and now feels as though she is walking with one foot in earthbound reality and the other foot in another dimension. She laughingly conceded that she doesn't always know just which side she's on, but said, "It is all magic and it is all so beautiful."

Charmaine has been working on a book about nature spirits, and she said that she had seen quite a number of the etheric entities in the Sedona area. According to her analysis of the beings:

> I have found them to be quite different from the ones I have met before in other places. I don't always see elementals. I wish I could. Nor can I tell

you how to see them. It is just when I'm particularly filled with an exquisite joy and love that they just suddenly appear . . . and they are as solid as you are.

The energies that Charmaine had discovered in Sedona were very strong and sometimes quite capricious. A few weeks ago, she said, she had been walking on rocks downhill when she suddenly stumbled.

> I turned a somersault in the air and landed on my face. I could have been badly hurt, but I was not injured in the slightest. At first I couldn't believe what had happened: A nature spirit had grabbed hold of me and taken care of me so I would not be hurt. The being had turned me over in the air, then set me down gently.

Whether or not it was Charmaine's intense interest in researching the nature spirits that attracted the entities to her energy, their intercession during what could have been a very nasty fall indicates their essential benign attitude toward humans.

A Medicine Woman Spots a Wee Person Unaware

A great Native American Medicine teacher told me that one day as she was sitting at the edge of a river, she glanced up to see a *puckwudjini*, a "little vanishing person," coming toward her. When their eyes made contact, the little person scowled and asked: "Can you see me?" And then he answered his own question: "You *can* see me!"

"Of course I can see you," she said, laughing. "I'm a Medicine teacher, a shaman, one who strives always to be at one with nature. I can always see you and your kind."

The wee person was persistent. "But only when we allow you to do so. I wasn't allowing you to see me, so you shouldn't have been able to."

The Medicine teacher shrugged. "Don't worry. I won't tell the people over there at the picnic table that you are here. But you better quickly be about your business, because I know the children at the swings have already spotted you."

Spotting Menehunes in the Home of a Kahuna

Maycelle Brown of San Francisco told me of the time when she was in Honolulu enjoying the pleasure of visiting with Morna Simeona, a hereditary Kahuna priestess and a teacher of Huna, the traditional Polynesian spiritual path, and encountered a couple of *menehunes*, the "little vanishing people" of Hawaii.

I heard the sound of giggling in Morna's kitchen, so I got up to see who it was, because I knew there were only the three of us women in the house. The door between rooms was of the swinging type with a small window at the top. I looked through the window and caught a glimpse of two little fellows darting in and out from under the sink. They sensed my presence and just disappeared.

Later, I sensed their presence in the dining room, but they didn't show themselves. When Morna and Shirley came downstairs, we sat and visited in the front room for a while, and I saw them again, leaning against Morna's knee and hanging around her chair like two shy, small boys. As we were saying our good-byes, they came over to me and leaned against me fondly.

Her Playmates Were Swirling, Colored Masses of Pure Energy

P.M.H. Atwater, who grew up in Idaho and is today an accomplished and successful writer and researcher of the near-death experience, may, as a child, have seen the nature spirits as they really are.

As a child, I could readily see, hear, and talk to other human souls; and I honestly believed that everyone else could, too. But it was when I went outdoors that the fun really began. I never really saw little *people*, not ever! But I did see colored vortexes of swirling, pulsating energy that I played with and watched. It is strange now, looking back, but I never had any desire to give them names or to place them in any kind of human role. It simply was not necessary to me for them even to have human forms. It was always all right for them simply to be what they were, and for me to be what I was. We didn't have to be models of each other to communicate or to share life.

Perhaps I really shouldn't call them "vortexes," either. Perhaps the best description would be to call them "energy masses," for that's exactly what they were—pure energy. They made little movements and sometimes big ones without the benefit of wind. They behaved in playful fashions, sometimes kicking up a little dust here and there, sometimes ducking under a leaf or parting the grass.

They had colors, sounds, and odor. Their colors, though, were not as the ones I see in the regular world around me. No, their colors were more like shimmering, translucent colors that you could taste! Each little energy mass created its own sounds that I am at a total loss to describe. Everything was so natural, so complete.

I enjoyed my little friends whenever I could, and when I couldn't, I enjoyed whatever I was doing. They were not "bigger than life" things to me—they were simply another part of life. They were not separate ever, but they were a part of my total existence. As I grew older, they did not disappear, but became less important. It was seeing other human souls, observing living numbers, and perceiving sounds that bounced like tiny cubes in the air that caused me trouble growing up. These things and others like them are what I quickly learned to be quiet about, for to talk about them became a "sin."

Pockets of Intelligent Energy Around the World

After many years of researching the enigma of float-ing balls of light, the wee people, and the concept of nature spirits, I very often find myself with more ques-tions than answers. It seems to me that throughout the world there are pockets of energy in which another order of intelligence exists. This intelligence may well be "pure energy masses" with the shape-shifting ca-pacity to appear as elves, brownies, devas, and other variations on the theme of an altered human image. In some instances, these pockets of intelligent energy may be directed or influenced by human intelligence; in other circumstances, this energy may direct and control—even possess—human intelligence.

In essence, these "nature spirits" may be the "Elder Race" or the "Old Ones" referred to in so many myths and legends. At the same time, these little swirling vortexes of intelligence comprise a companion species with which humankind has maintained at least a million-year interaction in a strange kind of symbiotic relationship. On occasion, humans have exploited the relationship, as in the classic "shoemaker and the elves" or "witch/wizard and familiar" kinds of arrangements.

Generally, the relationship between the companion species has been positive. When Scotland's Findhorn Community cooperated with the nature spirits to pro-duce marvelous fruits and vegetables out of rocky and barren soil, one of the community's members, Dorothy

McClean, was informed by the intelligences that they might be considered *Devas* (from the Sanskrit, meaning "shining ones"). Ms. McClean was further told by the Devas that they were of an order of evolution existing parallel to humankind and that these entities wielded vast archetypal formative forces that could energize the processes of nature. The "shining ones" also warned that too many modern-day humans had lost their contact with the nature spirits and with their sense of oneness with nature. Such a separation on the part of too much of humanity had greatly increased the very real danger of destroying the world.

David Spangler of Findhorn was told by the Devas that the beings recognized humankind as a necessary and vital part of the synergistic state of the planet, thus they were benignly concerned with human survival because it bore directly upon the survival of Earth. Spangler's impression of humankind's relationship to these entities is that we are "first cousins," very much like Homo sapiens and the ape. It was his understanding that we somehow had a common ancestor.

Don't Try to Manipulate the Nature Spirits

While so many people who work very close to nature have spoken of sensing entities cooperating with them in agricultural, forestry, or conservation projects, I must herewith issue a stern warning to those who are tempted to play wizard or sorcerer and seek to control these beings. If within the would-be sorcerer there should exist an innate psychological weakness or if that person should somehow suffer a severe psychological shock sometime during the course of the interaction with the nature spirits, then certain psychic barriers may crumble, enabling the entity to blend with human intelligence and to become a parasitic spirit supported by a host body. When this occurs, "elf" may become transformed to "demon" and the host body can be horribly used, even destroyed, by the intelligence that has become amalgamated with its own.

And, to repeat, while most encounters with the denizens of the Shadow World that we term nature spirits are benign, even benevolent, the most ancient of people have always understood that there are certain areas that the entities consider sacrosanct, special to them. While literal "fairy circles" may not exist, there are across this planet certain mounds, caves, creek areas, and forest clearings that have been staked out by the entities as their very own and the wise human, sensitively in touch with the natural environment, knows better than to trespass on such ground.

In certain cases on file in my office, a nature spirit may have considered a deserted house or barn its own. Generally, if the entity understands that a human wishes to occupy the dwelling place, it will quietly move out. At most, a token gift of fruits, nuts, or meal would compensate the spirit squatter and make it agree to move on to a more natural habitat. However, in some instances, humans have just walked into a particular situation at the wrong moment, and they can experience some trauma before squatting rights are straightened out and understood.

A Nature Spirit Had Moved into the Empty House Before They Did

Together with the return of her questionnaire, Lorrie Jastrow sent an account of an experience that occurred to her and her fiancé shortly before their marriage. They had gone to a movie, then decided to drive out to the tiny house in the Wisconsin countryside where they would live after they had celebrated their nuptials. Here is her astonishing record of what transpired on that terrible evening.

It was fun to go out there and plan our future. The house was on land that was too wooded to be good farmland, but we planned only to plant a small garden and Karl would continue his job in town.

Our only light that night was our flashlights. Since we wouldn't be moving in for another month or so, the landlord had yet to switch on the electricity. He had given us keys to the place, though, and he didn't mind that we would drive out there to dream about our future life together.

That night when we walked into the house, I had an eerie feeling that something was wrong, that we were not alone. Karl must have felt the same way as I did, because he kept looking over his shoulder, like he expected to catch sight of someone spying on us. "I'm going to have a look around," he said, trying to sound casual. I stayed right beside him. We walked through the house, and Karl grinned at me, as if he were apologizing for feeling uneasy in what would soon be our honeymoon cottage.

Then we heard a strange chattering, like some giant squirrel or chipmunk, coming from a dark corner in the room. It suddenly seemed so unreal, unearthly, and a strange coldness passed over my body. I told Karl that I wanted to leave, that I was frightened.

But before we could move toward the door, Karl suddenly threw his hands up over his head as if he were trying to grab at something behind him. His head seemed pulled backward and to one side. His mouth froze in a grimace of pain and fear, and his eyes rolled wildly. He lost his balance, fell to his knees, then to his side. He rolled madly on the floor, fighting and clawing the air around his neck.

I stood by helplessly, stunned with fear and bewilderment. Karl managed to struggle to his feet. His eyes bulged, and he gasped fiercely for each breath. Some unseen thing seemed to be strangling him.

He gasped out that we must run to the car, that I must drive. Somehow, we got out of the house with Karl stumbling, staggering as if something heavy and strong were perched atop his shoulders with a death grip about his throat. "I . . . can't get the damned thing off!" he gasped.

At last we got to the car. I got behind the wheel, and Karl told me to drive . . . fast. He was still trying to pry the invisible monster's hands from his throat.

I drove for about two miles down the road, and suddenly there was a blinding flash inside the car. A brilliant ball of fire about the size of a basketball shot ahead of our car, then veered sharply to the left and disappeared into a clump of trees. I did not stop until we were back in town. Karl lay gasping beside me, his head rolling limply on the back of the seat.

He did not speak until we were well inside the city limits. "It was some inhuman thing from the pits of hell. It was big, strong, and it would have killed me."

Lorrie Jastrow concluded her account by writing that although they returned to their small home in the country with some trepidation, they never again encountered that monstrous, invisible strangler that chattered like a giant rodent. Once the nature spirit had time to calm down and come to terms with the fact that humans were reclaiming the empty house, it moved on to another more appropriate dwelling. But it certainly did give Karl and Lorrie a piece of its mind before it did so.

People who leave their vacation homes empty for the major portion of the year also frequently suffer from a nature spirit developing a proprietary interest in what appears to be vacant property.

Whose Cabin Is It, Anyway?

Scott Halstead said that he and his family had vacationed in the same cabin in Vermont for the past twenty-two years. "We started vacationing in this cabin when Allan was two years old, and we always take the last two weeks in August," he stated in his account. "And for twenty-two years, we've had to share the cabin with *something* else."

Over the years Lynette and Scott Halstead said that there were numerous signs to indicate that some spirit entity was protective of the cabin. Some were kind of frightening. All of the family members complained from time to time of the feeling that someone was watching them. Items would disappear and reappear in bizarre places. And an eerie kind of scratching noise would often be heard issuing from within the walls.

Out of curiosity, they once wrote to the Wagners, a family they knew rented the cabin in July, and asked if they had ever noticed anything "peculiar" during their two-week stay.

"Beverly Wagner wrote right back and said, 'I imagine you're referring to the invisible live-in maid?'" Lynette laughed at the memory. "The Wagners had noticed some of the same numerous little things that we had, but once when they left a messy table after a party at the cabin, they woke up the next morning to discover that someone or something had stacked the dirty dishes in the sink and cleaned the table top. Jim Wagner jokingly said that it must be elves, so he left a bowl of oatmeal on the front step that night. The next

morning it was gone, but, of course, birds or some crit-
ter could have eaten it."

Scott and Lynette made a point to emphasize their
contention that although the "something else" sometimes frightened them, their sense of the entity was
that it was extremely protective of the cabin and the
grounds on which their cabin and others like it had
been built.

"The cabin and nine or ten others are situated on a
beautiful lake, and the caretaker, Charlie Bostford, does
a really fine job of maintaining everything in terrific
shape," Halstead said. "Charlie knows that there is
something kind of spooky going on around those cabins, but he usually just shrugs and says that it doesn't
bother him. It sometimes bothers his dogs, though.
He's got two big German shepherds, and I've seen
them cower and whine when neither Charlie nor anyone else was near them."

Lynette said that when their son Allan was around
four and their daughter Tonya was only a few months
old, Allan would say that he had a friend who was an
Indian guide. "If we were afraid that he might wander
off in the woods, he would say, 'Big Arrow won't let
me. He says that I have to stay near the cabins.' Who
could complain if his invisible playmate was also a
good babysitter?"

Lynette and Scott agreed that the most dramatic evidence of a guardian spirit looking over the cabin came
in 1985 when Allan was eleven and Tonya was seven
and the two started building a fire in the fireplace.

"Of course they thought they were doing something

nice for us," Lynette said. "Even though it was kind of chilly, Scott and I had gone swimming. The kids knew that we would be cold when we got out of the lake and a fire would feel good to us. Allan had watched his father building a fire for years, so he knew the basics, but he just kept piling on kindling. Tonya wouldn't be left out, so she was tossing newspapers and magazines onto the fire. Pretty soon they had a huge blaze roaring in that fireplace."

Shivering, clutching towels to their chilled bodies, Scott and Lynette stepped inside the cabin to see the colonial-style rag rugs in front of the fireplace on fire, the curtains to the side of the chimney ablaze, and another finger of flame moving across scattered newspapers toward the living room carpet.

"There was that moment of panic, when you just kind of scream and shout before your brain kicks in," Lynette said. "Allan and Tonya were standing against a wall, crying their heads off in fear."

And then, as strange as it may seem—as strange as it is for Scott and Lynette to attest to it—something started to beat out the flames.

"I'm standing there barefooted and soaked in my swim suit with a towel wrapped around me," Scott Halstead said. "I don't even have time to react, really, when I see something snuffing out the fire. More than beating out the flames, it's like something is smothering it, as if it is covering the fire with a big wet blanket. In minutes, what looked like it would be a major disaster has become a smoke-filled cabin, a couple of burned and scorched throw rugs, a blitzed curtain, and two crying kids."

Lynette said that she hugged Allan and Tonya and gave thanks to God, all attending angels, "and to whatever protective spirit looks out for the cabins."

When Allan was seventeen and Tonya thirteen, the two of them decided to try to make contact with Big Arrow through a Ouija board.

"This was not a good idea," Lynette said. "Scott and I were playing cards at another cabin, and when we got home, the kids were freaked. I guess a lot of really weird—and pretty obscene—stuff had come through and scared them spitless. For the rest of our vacation, Allan refused to sleep in the room that had been his for fifteen years, and he bunked out on the couch until it was time for us to leave."

Scott and Lynette commented that that summer had actually been Allan's last vacation with them at the cabin. The next year he graduated from high school and got a summer job before leaving for college. "After that it was college, a new job in Boston, marriage, kids, and visits only at holidays," Scott said. "Tonya vacationed with us until she graduated from college, so now it is just the two of us with Big Arrow or whoever watches over the place."

In all seriousness, both Scott and Lynette speculated that it could be the spirit of some Native American who cherished the environment around the lake and who kept a vigil over the cabins and their inhabitants, but they added, they had come to believe that the force, the energy, that loved the place so much was something more primeval.

"It's almost as if nature itself is somehow protective of the few remaining areas that we humans haven't covered over with concrete and erected shopping malls and gas stations on," Scott said. "Sometimes I would visualize some kind of elf or nature spirit sitting outside near the lake, looking across the beauty of this area toward the city and sighing, 'What fools these mortals be.'"

For centuries now, we humans, especially those of us who live next to the land, have sensed that there are truly sacred areas that must not be violated. In the next chapter we shall encounter the remarkably powerful entities from Shadow World that I have named the Deiform Spirits.

CHAPTER NINE

Sacred Places of the Deiform Spirits

Vincent Malone had an incredible story to tell me. He will not disclose exactly where the incidents that he described occurred, for he does not want anyone to undergo the traumatic experience that he barely managed to survive with his sanity intact. He shares an account of his ordeal so that others might profit from his mistake.

In 1982, Malone was vacationing in the Southwest at the home of a friend who owned a considerable amount of land.

"I suppose the desert country can grow on you," Malone said, "but to me, Zack had nothing but miles and miles of worthless land with nothing but cactus, scrawny shrubs, scorpions, and rattlesnakes. Give me the city, anytime."

Although he enjoyed catching up with his old buddy from the dismal days in Vietnam, there was little else to hold his interest during his seven-day visit other than the times when they would break out Zack's rifles and pistols and do some target shooting.

"I remember Zack telling me years ago that he had started collecting firearms when he was just a kid," Malone said. "He even had a bunch of old black powder, cap-and-ball muskets, and rifles. The one good thing about the desolate country he lived in was we could just step out his back door and start blasting away. Nothing against Zack's wife and his two sons who were home from college on vacation, but plinking away at targets was the most fun I had while I stayed there."

Early on in his visit, Malone wondered about hunting some wild game. Coyotes came up to the place every night to knock over the garbage pails, and their howling at night sometimes got downright spooky. And javelinas, the wild pigs, seemed plentiful.

"Got to keep an eye on those javelinas," Zack warned him. "The boars get pretty good-sized and they will charge you. They also get proprietary. One of our neighbors left his garage door open when he drove into town, and by the time he returned, a family of javelinas had taken over his garage and wouldn't let him back in. He had a terrible time getting them out."

Malone wondered why the neighbor didn't just shoot the wild pigs.

"We've got pretty strict hunting laws in this state," Zack told him. "The game wardens really watch out for out-of-season poachers and enforce limits. Plus, where I live here, there's another law in force that I don't mess with. I'm happy shooting cans and targets."

When Malone asked Zack what he meant by the "other law" in force, his friend looked away and became very silent.

Malone was puzzled by his friend's behavior and pushed him to explain. Zach took a long time to fill and tamp his pipe before he spoke. "Vince, I don't really remember you as being very religious, and what I'm about to tell you will probably sound flaky and weird to you. You know, the old Navajos, Apaches, Hopis, and Pueblos argued, fought, and skirmished over a lot of things, but they all agreed that there were special sections of this country that were sacred and were watched over by spirits that would take revenge on anyone who violated certain boundary lines."

Malone remembered wondering if Zack had been away from civilization too long. Old Native American tribal folklore was interesting to some folks, Malone acknowledged. He wasn't one of them.

Since Zack had grown silent again, Malone prompted him. "I guess what you're suggesting is that some spirit watches over the wildlife on your spread. Am I right?"

Zack nodded. "There's a canyon at the far end of my property that no one enters. Some people who did have lived to regret it. You may laugh, my friend, but out here in the desert, there are spirit beings and . . . things that you wouldn't understand unless—"

"Unless you were superstitious," Malone interjected, almost immediately regretting his rudeness to a faithful buddy who had slogged through the jungles and rice paddies of 'Nam with him.

"Unless you have opened your own spirit and learned to revere the desert, its wildlife, and all its powers," Zach corrected him. "Some say that the thing that watches over this patch of ground is a *Chindi*, a kind of guardian spirit that can shapeshift into any form it wishes to punish those who would violate the wildlife of this land. Not only can it assume any form, the *Chindi* can inhabit any living thing in its path of retribution."

Malone saw that his friend was serious, and he wondered how long a person would have to stay out here in the heat and the desolation before such primitive beliefs would begin to erode a rational mind.

The day before he was to leave the parched terrain with its scorpions, Gila monsters, mangy coyotes, tarantulas, rattlesnakes, and superstitions, Malone woke up to find himself alone in the ranchhouse. Zack and his wife had left early to drive into town to pick up some groceries for a farewell dinner for their guest.

Malone poured himself a cup of coffee from the pot left brewing on the stove and decided to step outside for some target shooting. "I was barely out the door when a small family of javelinas came grunting around the corner, making me nearly jump out of my walking shorts. I fired a couple shots in the air and they turned tail and ran. And that's when I got the idea."

Malone couldn't resist visualizing what a trophy a

javelina head would make hanging on the wall of his office. Talk about a conversation starter. And how macho would that be regarded in the big city, huh? How many warehouse managers had a javelina head on their office walls?

"I didn't know about which hunting season it was, but I figured if you shot a javelina or coyote on private property, it couldn't be any big deal," Malone reasoned.

Two young Hispanic men were working on Zack's yard, pulling weeds and grooming the place for the party that night. Malone would agree that he may sometimes have been foolhardy, but he was never a fool. He knew that a greenhorn like he was could easily get lost in the desert. He asked the two young men if they wanted to take a break and go target shooting with him farther away from the house.

"I think one of the kids was a mindreader and guessed what I was thinking," Malone said. "He shook his head and kept raking. The other grinned, told me what a good shot he was, and climbed in beside me in Zack's Jeep."

Then, according to Vincent Malone's account:

Tomas told me what I already knew about it being against the law to shoot the big cactus plants, but he really was a good shot picking off bits of debris and an occasional rattlesnake. We had been gone about forty-five minutes when we scared up fourteen or fifteen javelinas. I gave chase in the Jeep, and we pursued the herd until it ran into a small canyon. I stopped the Jeep and picked up the .30-.30 lever action Winchester from the backseat. Tomas' eyes got wide as silver dollars, and he asked me what I was going to do. I laughed and told him to tell me what it looked like I was going to do. I was going to bag me a trophy.

Tomas shouted at me not to do it. He even grabbed at my arm. I shook myself loose and glowered at him, warned him to step aside. Then the kid ran over to a large flat rock that rested against the side of the narrow path leading down into the canyon. He pointed to some old petroglyphs etched into the rock's face and told me that the signs warned all those who would trespass to turn and walk away. I laughed, figuring that I had discovered the haunted canyon that Zack had told me about.

Then, lurching up out of the canyon, snorting, stomping his hooves, came the largest javelina boar that I had ever seen, sporting two tusks the size of Bowie knives. It was the Big Daddy of all javelinas. With those tusks he could gut a buffalo. Hell, he could have gutted an elephant. He stood there right at the mouth of the little canyon, grunting, squealing, telling me in javelina language to get the hell off his property. I nailed him with a solid shot right between his eyes. But he only shook his head and started to come for me. I figured that his skull must be two inches thick. I fired another slug just beneath his large, gaping snout and that one made him squeal. A third bullet smashed his right foreleg. With that painful blow sending him reeling, he turned and ran back down into the canyon.

By this time, Tomas was curled into a fetal position in the Jeep and crying, shivering in fear. I told him that I had wounded the boar and that I would have to go into the canyon and finish him off. Tomas seemed hysterical, babbling about what I had done, the terrible crime that I had committed, how we would be punished terribly. I yelled at him, told him that a conscientious hunter never let a wounded animal die in pain. It was my obligation to finish the boar off.

But I walked from one end of the canyon to the other, and the only animal I found was a runty, diseased young javelina with three slugs in it. It was squealing feebly, blood bubbling out of its little snout, so I killed it with a head shot. I wondered where the massive boar had gone. And why this shriveled little runt had three slugs in its body in the same places where the big guy would have them.

I walked out of the canyon carrying the runt. It was no trophy for a big city warehouse manager to put on his office wall. I told Tomas that I would bury the wretched little thing, and he argued to leave it for the scavengers. At least by so doing I would not be violating the ways of nature any more than I had.

That night at his farewell party, Malone found himself treated worse than a leper. "People might have some pity for a leper's condition," Malone commented. "The folks Zack had invited for the party acted like they didn't want to come near me. It was as if they knew I was about to be struck by lightning and they didn't want to attract any bolts in their direction."

Obviously, Tomas had spread the word about Malone's violation of the sacred canyon and his shooting of the runty javelina.

"I spent the last night at my buddy's home alone in the guest room watching television," he said. "The party broke up before ten with everyone making excuses why they had to leave early."

Zack got up the next morning to see him off, but his friend's wife remained in their bedroom. "I wish you luck man," Zack told him. "Believe me, you're going to need it."

Malone got into the rental car feeling morose. He had often heard how even the best of friends could eventually drift apart because of lack of common interests and experiences. He guessed that was what had happened between Zack and him. After all, 'Nam was eleven years ago. A few cards and letters two or three times a year and a few beers at service reunions weren't really enough to keep a friendship percolating.

It was when Malone stopped for gas at the small town before heading back to the airport that he realized strange things were about to begin occurring in his life.

The old man at the pumps was cleaning his car's windshield when suddenly he leaned toward the glass and scowled at Malone. "Did you have to shoot it? Did you have to kill the little javelina? What a mighty hunter you are!"

Malone got out of the car to face the man. Had word spread from the party last night at Zack's place to the entire little community by the next morning? "What did you say to me?" Malone demanded of the elderly station owner.

The old man set down the bottle of window cleaner. "I said, I hope you enjoyed your stay here in the desert."

The man's wrinkled face was completely guileless as he gave Malone a friendly smile. Malone decided that his ears had played tricks on him.

But then there was the attendant at the check-in depot for the rental car. "Mighty hunter, are you?" the man at the desk sneered. "Shoot a poor little javelina. Must have taken some guts."

Before Malone could respond, the female clerk beside him fixed Malone with a fierce look and told him, "Get back to the big city where you belong. We don't want your kind of murdering trash out here."

"I didn't murder anyone or any—" Malone began to protest, but suddenly all four or five customers standing in line to rent cars looked at him with disdain and began to chant, "Murderer . . . murderer . . ."

Malone stated in his report of his bizarre experience,

> I literally ran out of the place. I felt like I was in some kind of waking nightmare. When I got on board the bus that would take me to the airport from the rental depot, the driver greeted me with an accusation of having slaughtered innocent wildlife. Everyone else on the bus looked at me as if I were a serial killer.
>
> When I stopped by the newsstand in the terminal, the woman behind the counter said, "I hear you're a really good shot. I hear you shot a poor little piggy."

I threw down a bill and walked away quickly with my newspaper. As I approached the security checkpoint, one of the guards spoke up and said, "Here comes the mighty hunter. Or is it the slayer of the innocent?"

Finally I was on board the 747, feeling on the edge of a nervous breakdown. Everything seemed all right until takeoff when the pilot said, "We are now leaving the desert country. Mr. Malone, I sincerely hope you enjoyed shooting that little runt." I looked at the passengers around me, but they seemed not to have heard.

Later, when the flight attendants brought the meal, I unwrapped the tinfoil around my serving dish and screamed. There on my plastic tray was the head of a small javelina. I covered my eyes, started to gag. One attendant handed me a vomit bag and another asked what was wrong. When I looked again at the tray, I saw that the meal was lasagna. I waved the vomit bag away, told the attendants I would be all right. But inwardly, I felt I was experiencing a nervous breakdown.

Vincent Malone said the torment did not end when he arrived at his destination. Nearly everyone he passed in the terminal turned to ask him such questions as, "How was the hunting?" "Did you bag your limit?" "Say, I hear you like to shoot living things, that right?"

Malone truly felt as if he were going insane. He stayed in his apartment throughout the entire weekend. He didn't even turn the television set back on after the anchor on the local newscast looked directly into the camera and said, "Vincent Malone does not respect the life force."

"I had heard about people losing touch with reality and thinking that people on the television were talking to them and that total strangers were speaking to them about personal matters," Malone said. "But I also remembered Zack telling me about the *Chindi*, the spirit that guarded the wildlife on that sacred ground, being able to assume any shape or to inhabit the form of any living thing to work its revenge. I guess I must really have angered it when I trespassed into that sacred canyon."

Things seemed better on Monday at work. There was only a message on his answering machine that warned him, "Respect all living things."

For nearly a year after the incident, Malone said, he would occasionally receive a telephone call in which an anonymous speaker would tell him to respect all the creatures of Earth. Once, on the subway, an elderly woman handed him a note that read, "Show kindness and respect to all living things."

What Vincent Malone learned with the most persistent kind of reinforcement is that there are areas of the planet that are held in great esteem by certain powerful entities and that are respected as sacred ground by all inhabitants who are aware and who wish to reside near those areas in peace.

Respecting the Sacred Areas of the Deiform Spirits

These entities from Shadow World that I have called Deiform Spirits have often been considered by the aboriginal people as gods and goddesses. While to place them in such a category overstates their position in the cosmic scheme of things, an appropriate respect for their energy recognizes their commitment to the guardianship of certain sacred areas.

The Deiform Spirits may be intelligent energy masses that have congealed in certain places due to the electromagnetic makeup of the terrain. Whatever their true nature and purpose may be, many men and women, such as Vincent Malone, have learned to take the intelligences very seriously. Many archaeologist and anthropologist acquaintances of mine have admitted that they have felt such presences during certain digs, and regardless of how their colleagues may have looked askance at them, they have conducted propitiatory rituals of appeasement to the entities.

The problem that most contemporary men and women have with the Deiform Spirits is that few modern disciplines teach respect for the beliefs of aboriginal people, and there is probably no facet of formal education that encourages an acceptance of the reality of the Shadow World. Without an awareness of the energies and entities that exist in a realm just beyond our three-dimensional boundaries, people may blunder into situations that place them in very bad trouble with the guardian spirits of sacred places.

Be Careful Where You
Build Your Houses and Roads

I receive many letters from people who have innocently constructed homes in the immediate proximity
of a tribal burial ground. Very often they are bothered
with strange disturbances that culminate in hearing
the sounds of drums and chanting. Their investiga-
tions into the area subsequently produce the revelation
that they inadvertently built their home on ground
hallowed by earlier residents of the environment.

One family, whom I'll call the McGowans, said that
almost immediately upon moving into their new
home, they experienced poltergeistic manifestations
and the unnerving sight of spirit forms projecting
themselves around the house. Only after doing some
research did they learn that their home had been built
on sacred ground, the very place where many tribespeople had been massacred and their bodies dumped
into a mass burial site.

Mrs. McGowan said that their home often received
violent slams at night, and they can often hear drums
beating. Other people, even nonbelievers in spirits,
have heard the drums and seen the forms of the entities.

"When the moon is full—especially in August, Sep-
tember, and October—you are more likely to hear the
drums," Mrs. McGowan said, "although we are certainly not devoid of them at other times. On some
nights we have been able to see what appears to be

masses of Indians carrying torches. They seem to be gathering for some kind of ceremony."

Native American shamans advise that it is always best to stay away from sacred ground when building houses or constructing highways. A few years ago I was told of a road crew that plowed through sacred burial grounds with a complete lack of sensitivity to the remains of an earlier culture.

According to a tribal shaman in the area, "When they unearthed the skulls and bones, some of the workers dressed up the grandfathers and grandmothers [the skeletons] in old clothes and made scarecrows out of them. One guy, a trucker, who hauled gravel to the construction site, put sunglasses on a skull and put it in the cab with him as his 'second driver.'"

Not long after such desecration, the workers began to suffer a series of accidents with the expensive machinery breaking down. At first these mishaps were only annoying, but as the disrespect for the skeletal remains continued, the level of accidents progressed to a number of close calls that were life-threatening.

By the time a group of traditional tribespeople arrived with a Medicine priest, the construction workers were ready to listen to them. Several of the workmen who had been on the site after dark had seen things that they could not explain, so these sightings, plus the series of accidents, convinced the construction bosses that the men should return the bones of the grandparents to the tribal representatives and permit them to rebury the remains in new ground that the priest had made sacred.

Gathering the Bones of the Grandparents for Reburial

For many years a friend from the Mesquaki (Fox) tribe has acted as the representative of a committee of traditional Native Americans that travels throughout the United States, seeking to persuade museums, curio shops, and private collectors to surrender the skeletal remains of the grandparents on display so that they might be returned to their respective tribes for sacred reburial.

As he explained, "We have no interest at all in collecting the arrowheads, pottery, and beadwork from the museums, the shops, the collectors. We have no more interest in these artifacts than any other American who might be curious about the history of this country. We only wish to rebury the skeletal remains that are languishing in Anglo museums. It is our desire to provide the grandparents with sacred interment in consecrated ground. We feel that this is no different from, let us say, a Christian who might not wish to see his grandparents' bones on display and who would wish to see them buried in consecrated, holy ground."

On more than one occasion, according to my friend, curio shops or small museums who denied his request later suffered a series of mysterious fires in the area in which the skeletal remains were being disrespectfully showcased.

"By all that I hold holy, I swear that neither I nor any human agency was responsible for these fires," my friend insisted. "It was the energy of the Great Mystery seeking to soften the hearts of the curators and shopkeepers. In a number of such cases, I received calls from those collectors who had at first refused my request, who were now asking me to *please* come back and remove the skeletons."

Beware of Buying Disrespectful Artifacts

Among the most vulgar acts of disrespect that has come to my attention are those reports of individuals who are using Native American skulls for ashtrays. It has been told to me that even the skull of the great Nez Perce Chief Joseph has been made into an ashtray for a dentist's office.

In 1992 I received a letter from a woman in Oklahoma, who told of the trouble that she and her husband experienced when he bought such a grisly artifact for his desk:

I never should have let Vernon buy that old Indian skull that someone made into an ashtray. And I could soon understand why that fellow at the roadside stand outside of Tulsa seemed so awfully anxious to get rid of it. I told Vernon it was tasteless and vulgar to have such an ugly grinning thing on his desk. Besides, I told him, those old Indians were human beings, too.

Vernon does a lot of paperwork for his business at home. The first night he came home and set that skull on his desk, he came back after supper to find important sheets of figures scattered around his office. He blamed it on some freak draft.

And then his computer started acting up. It just stopped doing what he wanted it to do. One time when he was working late on some important statistics, the computer blinked twice and erased every bit of input he had just spent the last eight hours inserting.

Then one night about a week after he had bought the godawful skull, I heard him screaming that his office was on fire. I came running in with the fire extinguisher and papers were burning every which way. Vernon swore he had no idea what had caused the fire. I blamed it on his terrible smoking habit, but he said that he had been careful to put out every butt in that horrible skull ashtray.

Later that same night while we were watching television, both of us felt the hair raise up on the back of our necks. We turned around at the same time to see this big Indian in full regalia standing beside the skull on Vernon's desk. The Indian didn't say anything, he just scowled and pointed at the skull ashtray. Then he disappeared.

Vernon, who had never even believed in Santa Claus or the Easter Bunny when he was a kid, sat up scared half to death all night. The next morning he couldn't get rid of that skull fast enough. He told me he tossed it in the river, and once he did, his office—and our lives—returned to normal.

Hounded by Mysterious Beings for Nearly Twenty Years

As I said earlier, many individuals are completely innocent of any deliberate act of disrespect to the sacred areas of the Deiform Spirits, but innocence of the spiritual laws is not seen as any excuse by the entities from the Shadow World.

Some years ago I received a fascinating account from a young professor in the graduate department of a major university. His adventure across the murky borders of Shadow World began when he was seventeen.

Jim Hunter's father had been a senior sales representative for an import company based in the South Pacific. The company was always shifting the family around, but from March 1964 to May of 1968, they had lived in New Zealand.

In March 1967, shortly after he had turned seventeen, Jim had gone on holiday at the beach near the little New Zealand ocean town of Kawhai and had been swimming around a section of shoreline that was not usually penetrated by tourists. It was here that he found a flat, smooth metallic object under a tidal rock. According to Jim Hunter:

> The object was oval-shaped, smooth, rounded at the edges, and engraved with peculiar symbols. It weighed about one pound, and when I found it, it had been tightly wedged between two tide-level boulders that were only exposed at low tide. The

object looked very old. Algae and other sea deposits encrusted it.

When such objects are found in New Zealand, they are most often taken for Maori relics, which are in high demand. Jim's father immediately advised him to take the oval-shaped object to a knowledgeable Maori to have it examined.

Two weeks went by, during which time the object passed from hand to hand among Maoris who were experienced in appraising the relics of their people. At last the consensus was delivered to Jim: The object did not come from any time in their culture and they did not recognize what it could be.

A man who represented himself as a journalist for the *New Zealand Herald* arrived at the Hunter home and claimed that he had heard of the object from a contact among the Maoris, and he asked if he might examine it. After a few minutes of study, he offered his opinion that the object was made of some kind of bronze alloy, and he asked permission to take it to Auckland and run some tests on it.

Jim denied the journalist's request, for his father had already spoken to a friend at the university in Christchurch about the possibility of having a metallurgical analysis run on the object. Jim could not later recall if such an analysis had ever been made, but he did remember that the curio ended up in a dresser drawer in their home in Te Awamutu, where it was to remain until his father received orders to move to New York in May of 1968. As Jim Hunter recalled,

That was when I first discovered that the object was missing. I knew very well the drawer in which it had rested for nearly a year, but when I came to pack it for moving, it was not there. It had disappeared.

I was very chagrined, and slightly suspicious of one or two friends who might have envied my find, but I had nothing to do but accept my loss.

As the Hunters waited for the flight from Auckland International Airport in May, Jim's parents were saying good-bye to some friends at some distance from him when he was approached by two young Polynesian types, who claimed to be from New Zealand Inland Revenue. They asked him if he were taking anything illegal out of the country, and they were especially interested in learning if he had any relics, art objects, or the like.

The two men acted in a very professional manner, and they soon intimidated me. I did my very best to explain that I had no relics in my possession, but then they insisted that I go with them to a hotel to undergo a private baggage check. It was at that point that I called for my father.

Father demanded to see their identification and asked why they couldn't examine my baggage right there in the airport. When their answers didn't make sense, Father summoned a patrolling constable to intervene. His mere arrival seemed to frighten the two men away, and they shuffled off without

another word. The whole incident seemed very
shady and frightening to me.

That fall, back in the United States, Jim Hunter en-
rolled in Columbia University for his freshman year.
Shortly after the term had begun, he was approached
by a middle-aged Italian art dealer who said that he
had heard that Jim had spent some time in New
Zealand and that he was interested in purchasing
any relics or curios that Jim might have brought with
him.

Although the alleged art dealer was polite and
businesslike, he was annoyingly persistent. In spite
of my repeated denials that I had any such relics to
sell him, the man approached me three times before
the winter holidays.

Through correspondence, I learned that three of
my closest friends in New Zealand had been questioned by men who seemed to fit the description of
the two who had attempted to search my luggage at
the airport. In one instance, the New Zealand police
had to be called in to block continued harassment.
In another case, a girl's life had been threatened.

According to their letters to me, each of my
friends had been questioned about whether or not I
had given them anything to keep before I left New
Zealand. They all used words like "spooky,"
"weird," and "creepy" to describe the men who had
persistently troubled them.

In 1970, Jim Hunter transferred to Stanford University. He had no sooner moved into his apartment and had the telephone installed when he received a call warning him never to return to New Zealand. During a later call, a woman with a high-pitched voice informed Hunter that he was being kept under surveillance by a group who felt that he had acted unjustly in the past by not returning things to their proper owners.

In 1972, Hunter decided to teach high school for a time before he continued with his graduate work. That summer, a few weeks before he was to begin his first job in the Sacramento school system, he was vacationing in San Francisco. Late one night, the telephone rang in his hotel room, and Hunter answered it to hear a man tell him that he had acted wisely by not returning to New Zealand. Hunter explained,

> You must understand what a quiet life I led as an undergraduate. Yet at both Columbia and Stanford I probably received *thirty or more* telephone calls from anonymous voices advising me not to return to New Zealand. In other instances, the voices reprimanded me for having taken something that did not belong to me.
>
> I didn't wear an armband declaring that I had lived in New Zealand, and I seldom discussed my life there with any but a few of my closest acquaintances. Who could possibly have cared about my finding that metallic slab? And who could possibly have taken such a long-term interest in me because

of a casual act committed a few days after my seventeenth birthday?

About the third day after classes had begun in the suburban community of Sacramento where Hunter had accepted a high school teaching position, a student unknown to him stopped by his classroom to say hello. Hunter knew that such an act was hardly unusual, since students will often do this to look over a new teacher, but from the first moment he stepped in the room, the boy acted strangely inquisitive.

I was astonished when the teenager stepped to the blackboard and drew the same design that I had first seen on the mysterious metallic object that I had found in New Zealand. He smiled at me, then asked if I knew what the symbols meant.

When I pressed him, in turn, for some answers, the boy erased the design, laughed, and said that he was just fooling around, that he didn't mean anything by it.

I never saw the kid again. I described him to a couple of the teachers and to a bunch of students, but no one was able to identify him. I doubt very much if he actually went to the school at all.

After four years of high school teaching, Jim Hunter was awarded a teaching assistantship at a major university and arrived in the fall of 1976 to begin his doctorate program.

I hadn't been at the university more than four days when someone rang my room and scolded me for taking things that didn't belong to me. The voice told me that I should never take anything from where I found it. It said that I should always leave things where they were. It went on to say that I had no right to act unjustly and to take things away from their proper owners.

At the time that Jim Hunter contacted me in the mid-1980s, he was receiving only an occasional mysterious telephone call in which the voice at the other end remonstrated with him for taking that strange metallic object from where he found it. As incredible as it may seem, the power of the angered Deiform Spirit was still punishing a young man for disturbing a sacred object nearly twenty years after he had innocently picked it up from its special place on a beach in New Zealand. Even though the mysterious artifact had not been in his possession for many years, his unintentional violation of a relic deemed holy by a Deiform Spirit had set in motion a retribution that, from Hunter's viewpoint, bordered on persecution.

When I hear of such encounters with Deiform Spirits, I think also of the reports that I receive from individuals who have met the spirits of Native Americans in sacred Medicine areas—or in their own homes—after removing some object from a sacred place. It is then that I hear the echo of the prophetic warning issued by Chief Seathe (Seattle) to the white men who cheated his people out of their lands with the Treaty of Point Elliott in 1855:

> Every part of this country is sacred to my people. Every hillside, every valley, every plain and grove has been hallowed by some fond memory or some sad experience. . . .
>
> When the last red man shall have perished from the earth and his memory from among the white men shall have become a myth, these shores will swarm with the invisible dead of my tribe. . . .
>
> At night when the streets of your cities and villages shall be silent, and you think them deserted, they will throng with the returning hosts that once filled and still love this beautiful land.
>
> The white man will never be alone. Let him be just and deal kindly with my people, for the dead are not altogether powerless. Dead, did I say? There is no death, only a change of worlds.

And for the powerful Deiform Spirits who keep watch over the sacredness of Mother Earth, there are no boundaries between our dimension of physical reality and the Shadow World.

CHAPTER TEN

Phantoms, Phantoms, Everywhere

On October 17, 1998, the London *Mirror* reported that Prince Edward and a film crew saw a ghost ship while filming the second installment of his "Crown and Country" television series on the Isle of Wight. According to Edward, he had been telling the story of the *HMS Eurydice*, a twenty-six-gun frigate that had capsized and sank in Sandown Bay during a blizzard in 1878. The crew had been discussing how they might illustrate the incident when a three-masted schooner suddenly appeared.

Excited to be able to film a vessel similar in appearance to the *HMS Eurydice*, the cameramen began to focus on the schooner. And then it disappeared.

Robin Bextor, the program's producer, told journalist Gerry Lovell that they had filmed the vessel for a while, then decided to wait so they could catch it sailing off into the horizon. "We were pleased at our stroke of luck at seeing it because it would save us time and money getting footage of a similar vessel. We took our eyes off it for a few minutes, but when we went to film it again, it had gone."

Officials of the Sail Training Association added to the mystery by saying that they knew of no vessel in the area at the time Edward and his television crew saw the ghost ship. The association stated that they did have two three-masted training ships, but on that particular week they were both away.

Prince Edward said that he was convinced that as far as ghosts were concerned, "there are too many stories, coincidences, occurrences, and strange happenings. There is definitely something out there . . . I cannot believe it is just people's imagination. There is more in it than that."

And in this particular sighting of a phantom ship, the television crew had the good fortune to have captured it on film.

Phantoms, Phantoms, Everywhere

Perhaps you could find yourself in a similar situation to that of Prince Edward—actually sighting an authentic phantom such as a ghost ship or a specter in a haunted room. Edward and his television crew found their ghost ship quite by accident—by just happening to be in the right place at the right time to witness a genuine paranormal phenomenon. It is possible for you to find yourself in such a position without going to sea or traveling far from home, for these United

States have accumulated a heavy population of phantoms.

Depending upon your disposition toward the unknown, you may either wish to avoid the following locations, or, since most of the entities listed below seem benign, you may be attracted to these haunted hotels and highways in order to encounter Shadow World in a more or less secure way.

The Old Stagecoach Inn in Waterbury, Vermont: Margaret Spencer, a wealthy, vivacious beauty who died in 1943 at the age of 98, haunts Room 2 of the Old Stagecoach Inn in Waterbury, Vermont. Margaret is often glimpsed in a wispy, white shawl, and she loves to play tricks on the inn's guests.

St. James Hotel, Cimarron, New Mexico: It would probably be best to avoid Room 18. Things get a little too wild in that room. But pick almost any other room in this 120-year-old hotel—a favorite of gunfighters in the 1880s—and you will probably find that you are sharing it with a phantom. According to yellowed newspaper accounts, twenty-six people have died violently at the St. James, and the dining room ceiling remains pockmarked with bullet holes. A quick perusal of the old guest register reads like a *Who's Who of the Wild West*: Billy the Kid, Pat Garrett, Bat Masterson, Black Jack Ketchum, Doc Holliday, Buffalo Bill Cody.

Bartenders and chefs in the hotel complain that food and crockery disappear from under their noses. Bottles and glasses float in the air and sometimes shatter in loud explosions. "A lot of gunfighters checked into this old hotel," a bartender exclaimed, "but their spirits have never got around to checking out!"

The Mission of San Antonio de Padua: There are guest accommodations in the old Mission of San Antonio de Padua, located in the central California mountains of the Santa Lucia range, thirty miles north of Paso Robles. Constructed in 1771, the Mission remains an enchanted, spiritual, haunted place. If you can make arrangements to stay overnight, you might very well catch sight of the ghosts of several monks, the benevolent spirit of Father John Baptist, and the mysterious entity that manifests as a headless woman on horseback.

The monks who reside in the Mission speak of having often seen a small colored cloud, about three feet square and about eight feet high above the tile roof over the women's guest quarters. The cloud changes color from white to green to blue, then yellow and red.

On numerous occasions in recent years, the Mission has been the scene of remarkable spiritual conversions and healings. And the monks speak of such miracles as the appearance of white and purple violets on certain graves within the courtyard.

Kennebunk Inn, Kennebunkport, Maine: This 200-year-old inn is haunted by a friendly ghost named Silas, who delights in levitating champagne glasses and tossing beer mugs around the bar. The phantom shade of Silas Perkins has haunted the Inn since his

demise in the eighteenth century, and weekend vaca-
tioners flock there in the hope of getting one of his
spiritual uplifts.

The Inns of Nantucket Island: According to hundreds of tourists, nearly any place of lodging near the
town's historic section harbors its share of unseen
guests. Even the Coast Guard station is haunted.

When author Peter Benchley was on the island
writing the book that would become the bestseller
Jaws, he encountered the ghost of an old man dressed
in eighteenth-century clothing. The entity sat in front
of a fireplace in a rocking chair—and Benchley insists
that he was not dreaming.

The Dorrington Hotel, Dorrington, California: The
ghost of Rebecca Dorrington walks at night in this
120-year-old hotel in the tiny High Sierra hamlet of
Dorrington. The town itself was named for Rebecca,
the Scottish bride of John Gardener, an 1850s home-
steader who also built the old hotel. Rebecca's eerie
nocturnal repertoire consists of banging doors open
and shut, flashing lights on and off, and shifting furniture about. Some guests have been "treated" to a
ghostly re-enactment of Rebecca's tumble down a back
stairwell, the accident that cost her her life in 1870.

Hotel Monte Vista, Flagstaff, Arizona: The picturesque old Monte Vista Hotel provides a marvelous
place for an overnight stay on the way to or from the
Grand Canyon. Guests who stay there may encounter

the "phantom bellboy," who knocks on doors and announces, "Room service," in a muffled voice. Others claim to have seen the wispy image of a woman strolling through an upstairs corridor.

Black Bear Inn, Elmwood, Wisconsin: If you're into UFOs, the ghostly lights that haunt our skies, spend a night in the Black Bear Inn in Elmwood, and you are almost guaranteed a UFO sighting. Elmwood, in the heart of the nation's dairyland, declares itself to be the "UFO Capital of the World." The townspeople claim to have witnessed so many unidentified aerial objects that they talk of building a landing strip for alien spacecraft.

The Brookdale Lodge in the Santa Cruz Mountains: The sprawling Brookdale Lodge, built in 1924 in the Santa Cruz Mountains near Boulder Creek, California, was a popular hideaway for gangland kingpins in the 1930s. Later, the Lodge was a favorite of film legends Marilyn Monroe, Joan Crawford, and Tyrone Power. The colorful inn, which features a brook running through the dining room, has a number of "cold spots," which indicate haunted areas. The most frequently sighted spirit entity is that of a small girl dressed very formally in 1940s-style clothing. The ghost is thought to be that of the five-year-old who drowned in the brook sometime in the late 1940s.

San Carlos Hotel, Phoenix, Arizona: Guests have complained about the noisy children in the halls.

When they are informed that there are no children running about unattended, some annoyed patrons have set about trying to prove they aren't going crazy by catching the shouting, squealing, laughing kids who are disturbing their relaxation and sleep. Some frustrated guests who have nearly grabbed one of the little rascals have been astonished to see the child disappear before their eyes. The only explanation that some investigators have offered for this phenomena is the fact that the old San Carlos Hotel was built sometime in the late 1920s on the sight of Phoenix's first adobe elementary school. Perhaps psychically sensitive guests are hearing and seeing the ghosts of schoolchildren from long ago.

The Horton Grand Hotel in San Diego: There are so many ghosts at the historic old Horton Grand Hotel in San Diego that the entities often get together and hold dances. A woman who lived at the hotel for two years claimed to have watched a group of fifteen to twenty ghosts dressed in the style of the 1890s, having a dance in the third-floor ballroom.

It was only after she had watched them for a while that Shelly Deegan realized that there was something very strange about the costumed dancers. No one paid the slightest attention to her. Everyone appeared to ignore her when she spoke. Then she noticed that there was something very eerie about their eyes, kind of dark and hollow.

The ghostly figures didn't seem to mind the intrusion of her physical presence. Ms. Deegan wondered if she were observing the re-creation of some past scene that had once occurred in the hotel. She remembered that they swung their partners round and round and seemed to be having a great time.

Room 309 receives the most nominations for "most haunted" in the Horton Grand. Research has revealed that a gambler named Roger Whittaker was murdered in that room in the 1880s.

Dan Pearson, the owner of the Horton Grand, said that he first became aware that there were strange things happening in Room 309 when he brought workmen in to renovate it in 1986. Later, as Pearson walked by the room with a psychically talented friend, the man stopped suddenly and said, "There's something going on in that room! I feel it strongly!"

Three months later, Pearson said that a guest at the hotel staying in Room 309 found her young daughter carrying on an animated conversation with someone else in the room. "Don't you see him, Mommy?" the girl asked incredulously. "Don't you see the man in our room?"

Our son-in-law, a media specialist, was recently in San Diego filming some of the unique architecture of various structures, when one of his technicians shared an experience when he stayed at the Horton Grand. "He called the front desk to complain that the people above him were making too much noise, as if they were marching up and down the hall. The front desk clerk responded, 'Sir, there is no floor above you. Perhaps you should have read the diary on the mantle.' The technician checked and found the diary filled with guest experiences with ghosts through the years at the Horton Grand."

In another of San Diego's haunted hotels, the El Coronado, where our son-in-law and his crew were filming a convention, he said that one of his technicians reluctantly admitted that an invisible someone had brushed against him when no one was around. After they had completed filming the function they were assigned to cover, the entire crew heard strange booming noises coming from a balcony loft area where there was no living, visible person.

The Whaley House in Old San Diego: Old San Diego is the birthplace of California. On Presidio Hill, Father Junipero Serra established the mission of San Diego de Alcala on July 16, 1769. In the early 1820s, a small Mexican community was formed that by 1835 had evolved to El Pueblo San Diego. Because it was the site of the first permanent Spanish settlement on the California coast, San Diego is as significant to the Pacific heritage of the United States as is Jamestown, the first English settlement in Virginia Colony, to our Atlantic ancestry. The first U.S. flag was raised on Old San Diego's tree-lined plaza in 1846.

Not only is Old San Diego one of the most haunted places in North America, but the Whaley House, constructed in 1857, just might be one of the most haunted mansions. June Reading, the amicable and knowledgeable director of the Whaley House, told us that immediately after its completion by Thomas Whaley the mansion became the center of business, government, and social affairs in Old San Diego. The oldest brick house in Southern California, the mansion served as a courthouse, a courtroom, a theater, and a boarding house—as well as the family home of Thomas and Anna Whaley and their children. Although guests can no longer stay overnight in the Whaley House, it is still possible to tour the mansion.

Almost every facet of haunting phenomena has been observed or encountered in this mansion. Footsteps have been heard in the master bedroom and on the stairs. Windows, even when fastened down with three four-inch bolts on each side, have opened of their own volition, often in the middle of the night, triggering the burglar alarms.

As they tour the mansion, people have often smelled cooking odors, Anna's sweet-scented perfume, and Thomas's favorite Havana cigars. Screams have frequently been heard echoing through the upstairs rooms, as well as the sound of girlish giggles and the rattling of doorknobs. Many people have heard the piano playing in the mansion's music room and the milling about of ghostly crowds in the courtroom. The ethereal images of Thomas and Anna Whaley have been seen on numerous occasions.

June Reading told us that in 1964 the popular television talk show host Regis Philbin and a friend saw Anna Whaley as they sat on the Andrew Jackson sofa at 2:30 A.M. The spectral image floated from the study through the music room, and into the parlor. At that moment, Philbin, in nervous excitement, "dissolved" the apparition with the beam of his flashlight. Since that time, Mrs. Reading said, night visits to the Whaley mansion have not been permitted.

Numerous photographs of spirit phenomena have been taken over the years in Whaley House. Sherry was able to capture on film a ghostly materialization of the noose that hanged Yankee Jim Robinson, a renegade who was executed on the site of what would later become the arch between the music room and the living room in the Whaley House.

Phantom Hitchhikers and Ghostly Vehicles

As you are driving to keep your rendezvous with a ghost in a hotel room, you might encounter a phantom on any one of a number of haunted highways.

The Misty Miss Latta on Arkansas Highway 64: Drive the lonely stretch of Arkansas Highway 64, especially on a rainy night, and area residents swear that you will be likely to sight the tormented spirit of Laura Starr Latta, who died a month before her twentieth birthday in 1899. Motorists have claimed to have seen Laura's small, frail frame inside a white nightgown standing on the side of the road across from the cemetery where her body lies. Some old stories say that Laura was accosted by a gang and beaten to death on the way to her wedding. Others say that she was killed by a runaway wagon or murdered by a bizarre cult.

All that is known for certain is that she died a month before her twentieth birthday in 1899.

The inscription on her tombstone reads GENTLE STRANGER PASSING BY. AS YOU ARE NOW, ONCE WAS I. AS I AM NOW, SO YOU MUST BE. PREPARE YOURSELF TO FOLLOW ME.

The Lady of the Lake, White Rock Lake, Texas: Most of the reports of the apparition of the Lady of the Lake come from lovers' lane couples or late-night drivers who see her appear along the side of the road. Local folklore says that she is the ghost of a woman who was drowned accidentally—or on purpose—in White Rock Lake.

According to some who have encountered her "face to face," the phantom appears to be jealous of young lovers and wishes to frighten them out of their amorous activities. One young man said that he would never forget the sight of the shimmering ghost staring in the car window at him and his frightened date. Drivers who have stopped to help what they believed to have been a woman in trouble, say that she leaves only a puddle of water where she had stood at the side of the road.

Resurrection Mary, Archer Avenue, South Side of Chicago: Chicago paranormal researcher Richard Crowe has quite a file on Resurrection Mary, a beautiful phantom hitchhiker: "She was buried in Resurrection Cemetery on Archer Avenue on the South Side of Chicago, which is where she gets her nickname. During the 1930s and 1940s, Mary was often picked up at dances by various people. She would ask for a ride toward Resurrection Cemetery, saying that she lived down that way. As people drove her home, she would yell at them to stop in front of the cemetery gates. She would get out of the car, run across the road, and dematerialize at the gate."

Crowe mentioned a recent report wherein two young men were fascinated by watching this beautiful blonde dance by them, but when she passed near them they got the strangest sensation.

"That night when they got home, they told their father about this woman," Crowe continued. "They'd never heard of Resurrection Mary, but their father recognized her by the description they provided. I investigated and found out that a week before this sighting, Mary had been seen dancing around the cemetery's fence."

Crowe told me that he had at least seven first-person accounts of people who have had Mary open their car doors and jump in, but he had only one first-person account of someone who met her at a dance and followed up by going to the street address she gave him. According to the man's report:

> She sat in the front with the driver and me. When we approached the front gate at Resurrection Cemetery, she asked us to stop and let her out. It was a few minutes before midnight. We protested, saying she couldn't possibly live there. She said, "I know. But I have to get out." So being gentlemen and she being so beautiful, we let her out, and she left

without saying anything. It was dark. She crossed the road running, and as she approached the gate, she disappeared.

She had given me her name and address, so early Monday morning, all three of us guys came to the number and street in the stockyards area. We climbed the front steps to her home. We rang and knocked on the door. The mother opened the door, and lo and behold, the girl's color picture was on the piano, looking right at us. The mother said she was dead. We told her our story and left.

My friends and I did not pursue the matter any more, and we haven't seen her again. All three of us went into the service thereafter and lost contact with each other.

Route 666—Arizona's Devil's Road: Although U.S. Route 666 will soon be officially known as U.S. Route 191, the legend of Camino del Diablo, "the Devil's Road," will long be remembered. According to numerous eyewitness accounts, on nights of the full moon, a black, 1930s vintage Pierce-Arrow roadster has appeared and run scores of cars, trucks, and motorcycles off the road. The ghostly automobile has been linked to at least five deaths.

Dr. Avery Teicher of Phoenix has spent ten years documenting reports of the phantom Pierce-Arrow and howling hellhounds that materialize to terrorize anyone foolhardy enough to pull off Route 666 and admire the desert landscape. According to Dr. Teicher, two members of a biker gang had both of their arms chewed off and a third had 90 percent of his face eaten away by the ghost dogs.

The least threatening of all reports from the Devil's Highway are those of a phantom female hitchhiker, who vanishes whenever someone stops to give her a ride.

The Phantom of Theresa Molnar Haunts an Entire Community

Folks frequently encounter Theresa Molnar in the small Nebraska town where she lived all of her life. People meet her out walking on the country roads that wend their way through the rich farmlands. She is regularly seen seated in one of the back pews whenever the old Methodist church has an evening service, especially during the religious holidays. On some occasions, Theresa even shows up unannounced in people's homes, often taking them quite by surprise and scaring the bejabbers out of them. You see, Theresa Molnar has been dead now for over eighty years.

As with all phantoms, there is a legend behind the ghostly appearances of Theresa Molnar.

In June 1914, Theresa was to be married to Lee Hollinger, a wealthy young farmer in his early twenties who had courted the beautiful redhead since she was a junior in high school. Although she had great affection for Lee, Theresa had plans to leave the tiny Nebraska village and travel to Omaha or Chicago and attend business school. She wanted some kind of career for herself, and she really didn't want to be a farmer's wife. Although it was daring for a woman of her day, Theresa really hoped to become self-sufficient.

But then, just before graduation from high school in May 1911, her mother became very ill. As the oldest child in the Molnar family, she was needed at home to cook for her father and her three younger brothers and two sisters. Her mother's crisis passed, but she was left weakened and somewhat of an invalid.

Theresa never got on the train for Chicago or Omaha; and finally at age twenty, when she could no longer keep her patient suitor's passions at bay, she had agreed to marry Lee in a big church wedding in June.

In December 1913, after the Methodist Church's annual Sunday School Christmas pageant, Theresa developed pneumonia and after two weeks of high fever and terrible discomfort, her lungs gave out and she died.

Lee Hollinger went through an awful time of grief and despair. His parents, Sam and Martha, kept a close watch on him for fear that he might commit suicide, so deep was his depression over losing his beloved Theresa.

That spring, however, no one in either family or in the small village thought it improper when Lee began to call upon Belia Molnar, Theresa's eighteen-year-old sister. The entire little Nebraska town had grieved along with Lee when Theresa had died so tragically, and now everyone seemed to approve of his courting of Belia.

And it wouldn't be as if he was falling in love with her because she so strongly resembled her older sister. Belia was, in fact, almost the complete physical and emotional opposite of Theresa. Belia was blonde, tall and slender, of a vivacious personality, and she loved to sing and dance. Theresa had flaming red hair, was a bit shorter and more full bodied, of a quiet and serious demeanor, and she loved to read and work at various handicrafts.

The only one in the entire village who had second thoughts about Lee's earnest courtship of Belia was Belia herself. She had adored her older sister, and she felt guilty when she realized that Lee was falling in love with her. She had felt that it was wonderful when they began keeping company to console one another over Theresa's death, but she had deep feelings that Lee was being unfaithful to the memory of her sister. Finally, after many late-night discussions with her mother and their minister, Belia began to acknowledge the feelings of respect and love that she had toward Lee.

In June of 1915, nearly eighteen months after Theresa's death, Belia Molnar was to marry Lee Hollinger on a sunny Saturday afternoon. As they had planned to do with their older daughter Theresa, George and Edith Molnar wanted the best and happiest of weddings for Belia.

After the ceremony at the Methodist Church, they made plans to move the festivities to the town hall so everyone in the village who wished to attend might come and give their congratulations to the bride and groom. And the Molnars made it clear that no one had to be in any hurry to leave. This would be a party with lots of cider and beer and a really good polka band, so folks could stay and dance all night if they so desired.

As the story goes, it was close to eleven o'clock, rather a late hour in those days, when Belia, who had just finished a lively polka with her uncle, paused to catch her breath and just happened to glance out the open window behind her mother. Her scream of fear silenced the band and the entire wedding party.

As Belia's features paled and turned a ghastly white, she pointed a trembling forefinger toward the window.

All those present who were near enough to the bride to witness her sudden fright followed her gesture, and they were shocked to see the clear image of Theresa Molnar standing there outside the window looking in at the festivities. When her mother, Edith Molnar, beheld the countenance of her deceased older daughter, she emitted a long, piercing wail, then collapsed into the arms of a friend.

According to the old stories, Theresa Molnar was dressed in the white shroud in which she had been buried. Most of the witnesses present that wedding night state that her stark white features bore an expression of great sadness.

Some accounts state that the spectre pointed an accusatory finger at Lee Hollinger. Others say that the ghost glared at Belia and called out her name in a frightening, sepulchral voice.

All witnesses agreed that everyone at the party stood stock still, eyes widened, mouths open in speechless shock and horror as everyone perceived the ghost of Theresa Molnar at the open window.

At last the bride's father shook himself free of the terrible spell and bellowed his rage at what he believed must be a cruel trick that some thoughtless prankster had sought to work on Belia and Lee. In his fury, he ran outside, cursing that he would put an end to such a tasteless and vicious prank. A good many male guests ran after the maddened father, some to restrain him and others to shout their encouragement of his grabbing and giving a good shaking to so vicious a trickster.

In the bright moonlight, George Molnar and his small posse of townsfolk could see the white-clad figure of a woman moving ahead of them. Molnar and several others shouted at the woman to stop, but she continued on a course that led directly to the town cemetery.

With the men in hot pursuit, the ghostly figure finally stopped when she stood beside the gravestone of Theresa Molnar. Then, in full view of George Molnar and his friends, she disappeared.

At that point, when he fully comprehended the incredible reality that he had been chasing and cursing the spirit of his deceased daughter, George dropped to his knees and began to weep and babble hysterically. Some of the men ran in fear back to the town hall.

One of Molnar's best friends stayed to help him regain his composure, and two other men, determined rationalists, remained behind to search the cemetery for any trace that a physical, flesh-and-blood woman might have somehow eluded them. They found not a single clue that could point to anything other than the materialization of Theresa Molnar's spirit.

Back at the town hall, the once lively and happy wedding party had deteriorated into a state of complete chaos.

Belia was in a state of shock, and a number of elderly ladies were hysterical. Lee was concerned that his elderly father had suffered a heart attack, and he had left to summon a doctor in a nearby larger community. The wedding dance and the celebration had ended in turmoil and confusion.

Belia never recovered from seeing Theresa's apparition at the window. She went home with her parents that night, and she never truly became Lee Hollinger's wife. She never spent a single night with him, and their marriage was never consummated. The ghostly image of her sister at the window had so filled Belia with guilt and an awful sense of betrayal that she lived in a constant fear that the accusing specter of Theresa would once again return and appear before her.

Refusing most days to eat or to drink, Belia simply wasted away, and within six months after the ghostly manifestation at the wedding dance, she joined Theresa in death.

Perhaps Belia's tortured soul had reasoned that the only way in which she could rectify matters with her sister was to die, thereby removing herself from Lee's

arms in the same manner that Theresa had been taken
from his embrace. Once such a suggestion had been
implanted in Belia's unconscious mind, she slowly
began to withdraw from life.

And once the many witnesses to Theresa's ghostly
appearance at the town hall shared their shocking encounter with their friends and relatives, it is little wonder that the number of those men and women who
would claim to see her sorrowful spirit suddenly increased by a quantum leap. Perhaps there actually
were continued authentic manifestations of the spirit
of Theresa Molnar, but it would not be long before
those who wished to see her specter or those who
feared to see it had projected enough psychic energy
into the original experience on Belia's wedding day to
create a phantom marionette that will continue to exist
as long as there are those who have a desire or a need
on a conscious or unconscious level to perceive such a
materialization.

For those readers who might wonder why after all
these years the townspeople continue to see the phantom entity of Theresa and not the ghost of Belia, the
story goes that Theresa's spirit is the restless one, for it
seeks her sister in the streets and houses of the small
Nebraska town so that she can apologize for disrupt-
ing Belia's marriage to Lee Hollinger.

According to tradition, the phantom is often heard
to ask those whom it encounters, "Have you seen
Belia?"

If you wish to be able to leave without the entity attaching itself to you for the remainder of the evening, you will answer, "Yes, she rests well and is at peace."

And with those words, the apparition of Theresa Molnar will disappear—and leave you in peace.

Trying to Identify the Players without a Clearly Defined Program

Such phantoms as that of Theresa Molnar have been seen by so many people over so many years that the initial phenomena may literally have begun to take on independent existences of their own, responding to the fears and expectations of its human audience and drawing regenerative energy from that same gathering of witnesses and believers.

In other instances, many so-called "haunted" houses and other sites contain no spirit beings, no entities from the Shadow World at all. In certain homes such powerfully charged human emotions as hate, fear, and pain have somehow impressed their energy into the natural environment and continue to broadcast impressions that may be perceived again and again by the psychically sensitive as if they were images on a loop of motion picture film that keeps being rerun in a projector.

To make things even more complicated, in certain cases the human mind can project fears and expectations upon a location and energize a haunting into being where no prior entity had existed. The psyche of many men and women can empower a phantom into a twilight zone of reality. Such is quite likely the case at the Yaquina Bay Lighthouse in Newport, Oregon. The lighthouse was built in 1871 and used for only three years until the Yaquina Head lighthouse was constructed.

According to the legend, one dark and stormy night a hundred years ago a group of teenagers crept into the abandoned lighthouse to explore its empty hallways, but one of them never came out. All that was left of one of the young ladies was her bloody handkerchief at the bottom of the third-floor staircase.

Ever since that girl met her mysterious fate in the lighthouse, people have seen an eerie light in the upstairs window and heard cries and moans issuing from the darkened interior.

In November 1998, Cathy Kessinger, writing in *Mid-Valley Sunday*, quoted Walt Muse, who oversees the lighthouse for the state parks department, as stating that there wasn't a "shred of evidence to support the spooky tale of the young woman who disappeared, leaving only a bloody handkerchief and a few drops of blood behind."

Muse said that he had heard all the stories about people seeing lights on in the lighthouse and hearing and seeing strange things to support the legend. He himself was surprised one night to see a single light in the third-floor window. After a careful examination, he concluded that the source of illumination must have been "light escaping from the beacon above."

Muse said that he is continually surprised by tourists who want to visit the haunted lighthouse. As he stands by, he often hears people saying that they "feel something" within its walls. "People have sent pictures they took while touring the lighthouse [that] show something passing in front of the camera, like an apparition."

As in so many instances of reported phantom beings, not only have the expectations of hundreds of people created a spirit and a mysterious light at the Yaquina Bay Lighthouse, they have kept it alive for over one hundred years by feeding it with their collective psychic energy. Although we have seen throughout this book that humankind is part of a larger community of intelligences, a complex hierarchy of powers and principalities both physical and nonphysical, we must always exercise caution that we do not populate the outer fringes of Shadow World with creatures of our own making.

CHAPTER ELEVEN

Preparing for Unexpected Visitors from Shadow World

Suspense writer David Christianson's friends always chided him that he should write about the unsolved mystery in his own family. Of course, David (the pseudonym we're giving a writer of stories of true crime and the mysterious) knew that they were referring to the strange disappearance of his sister Kristen, who vanished without a trace on April 30, 1967.

David had been twelve when his beautiful seventeen-year-old sister walked out of the family's front door in their small Minnesota town and disappeared into oblivion. He had to admit that he had often thought about turning the drama of his family's real-life tragedy into fiction, but he felt to do so would only bring back a lot of really bad memories.

David's account for my research files begins on April 30 a few years ago when his mother, Carol, called him on the anniversary of his sister's disappearance and asked that he drive out to their home before he started work that day. For many years they had held a family memorial service on the anniversary of Kristen's disappearance, and he assumed that his parents now regretted their abandoning the long-established observance and wished to spend a few moments together in honor of her memory. His mother quietly ushered him through the kitchen and into the living room.

David could see that she had been crying, but he sensed a much greater disturbance in her manner. He was quite unprepared for the condition in which he found his father.

Jacob Christianson was a man who never gave evidence of any physical, mental, or emotional weakness. When Kristen and David were kids, they thought their tall, strong father was the last of the Vikings. Yet now he sat slumped in his big leather chair, his eyes red and puffy from crying, his gray hair mussed, his clothes looking disheveled and slept in.

"David," he spoke in a harsh, croaking voice that betrayed a lack of sleep, "what it says in the Bible about powers and principalities is really true. There really are spirits that wander under the midnight moon."

Almost as shocking for David as seeing his father in such a rumpled and emotional state was hearing him mumbling about dark spirits. He wondered what the Bible's admonition to beware of unseen adversaries had to do with making his father so distraught.

David thought back to catechism class when he was thirteen. The scriptural passage that so concerned his father had been one of the verses that he had had to memorize to be a member in good standing in the Lutheran Church. The apostle Paul, writing to the Ephesians, chapter six, verse twelve: *"For we are not contending against flesh and blood, but against the principalities, against the powers, against the world rulers of this present darkness, against the spiritual hosts of wickedness in the heavenly places."*

"You still go to church, don't you?" Jacob suddenly wanted to know. "You, Emily, and the kids? What with Emily being a psychology teacher and all, she doesn't just rationalize away religion, does she?"

It was a tiresome discussion that they had had many times before. Although surely a spiritual person, Emily's belief structures were rather far from the rigid fundamentalism of Jacob Christianson.

David sat down on the sofa. It was certain that he would be staying awhile. He accepted the cup of coffee that his mother offered him. He wished that she would have warned him that Dad was acting so strangely.

Jacob shuddered, then suddenly cried out, "Oh, dear God, what if it really was Kristen? What if through some miracle . . ." He buried his face in his hands in an attempt to regain composure.

David knew that he should say or do something, but he was at a loss. This was so unlike the family patriarch. His father was a big, rugged man, still in good physical condition from a lifetime of hard work on the farm.

His mother spoke for the first time since he had arrived. "Your father's been upset since early this morning. You remember that it was twenty-six years ago yesterday that Kristen disappeared."

Remember? Kristen's disappearance had become their family's pivotal experience.

Every holiday, they set a place at the family table for her. For years, they had held a memorial service for her on the anniversary of her disappearance. David had worshipped his big sister, certain that she was the most beautiful, kind, and loving girl on the planet.

He looked at the photos lining the fireplace mantel. Kristen in her cheerleading outfit. Kristen in her drum majorette uniform. Kristen at age eleven with a six-year-old David. Kristen and David in Halloween costumes about to go trick-or-treating. Kristen dressed as an angel for the 1966 Christmas pageant at St. Olaf Church—her last Christmas with the family.

His father saw that the photographs had captured his attention. "At first I thought maybe I wasn't kind enough to her," he said, as if making an awful confession.

"Jacob," his mother protested, "what are you talking about? You were always kind to Kristen."

Jacob made a terrible gasping sound. "Last night Kristen came to the door, and she wouldn't come in! Can you imagine how that makes me feel?"

There was a terrible sinking feeling in David's stomach. Was his father's behavior the start of a mental and physical decline?

David had friends with parents the ages of his own who had spoken of a mother or a father who had never been sick a day in his or her life suddenly becoming very ill and dying within months. Or worse, being committed to an old folks' home to live out their last years in a kind of helpless, shadowy mental fog, talking to people no one else perceived, or seeing loved ones long gone.

"Dad," David said softly, "you know that Kristen has been gone for twenty-six years now."

He nodded his head, blowing his nose in a soiled handkerchief before answering. "She was here last night."

"Dad, you know that can't be so," Carol said gently. "We lost our Kristen . . . years ago."

Carol Christianson had been thirty-nine and Jacob forty-two when their lovely daughter walked out the door and never came back. She rose from the couch and walked to her husband's chair with a box of tissues. Tears welled in her own eyes as she placed an arm over his shoulders. "We so wanted our beautiful Kristen to come back home. But she never did, dear. She just never did."

Jacob accepted a tissue and wiped his nose. "But maybe she found her way home at last."

David leaned back heavily against the cushions of the couch. "Okay, Dad," he said, "please tell Mom and me what happened."

Jacob said that he had been sitting up late reading when he heard a soft knocking at the door. He glanced at his wristwatch and saw that it was nearly two o'clock. Wondering who could be out and about at such an hour, he cautiously opened the door and was startled to see Kristen, his lost daughter, standing there on the front porch.

"I smiled and started to step aside, rejoicing at her return," he said, his reddened eyes once again brimming with tears. "She looked just like she did when she disappeared. She was always so pretty . . . so pretty. And she stood there on the porch saying over and over, 'Daddy, I've come back to you.'"

At last David understood what all the talk about powers and principalities had been about. "Dad, it was just a dream. You fell asleep reading. You had probably been thinking about Kristen. She would have to have been in your mind. It was April thirtieth."

His mother agreed. "David is surely right. We used to hold a little memorial service for her on that night. Maybe you were feeling sad because we no longer do so. You know, it's not as if we have forgotten Kristen. It's just that we decided we must all move on."

In his mind David saw beautiful blonde Kristen on that long-ago sunny April afternoon. They had been listening to her new Beatles album and singing along with the lyrics as best they could. To his twelve-year-old eyes, Kristen was the most gorgeous girl who had ever lived. She was the peerless Queen of the Universe.

She had glanced at her wristwatch and said that she was going out for a little while. She had to pick something up at the drugstore in town. She promised to return in plenty of time to take him to see *Bonnie and Clyde* at the drive-in. Their mom and dad said that it was too violent for a twelve-year-old, but Kristen had said that she would take him. She would be back no later than seven.

By ten o'clock that night, everyone in the family was worried and concerned about Kristen. By midnight, everyone was frantic. Kristen always called if she were delayed in returning home by even five minutes. When they drove into town, they found her car parked in front of Holman's Drugstore, but there was no one around who had seen her anywhere. Their next stop was the police station.

At first, David was angry at her for making him miss the movie. Then came the days of walking through fields and forests, searching, searching—followed by the weeks of wanting never to give up, the months of praying she was alive somewhere, the years of never knowing what her true fate had been. David had never quite managed to purge himself of the guilt of having initially felt cheated out of seeing *Bonnie and Clyde*. He had, in fact, made it a point of never seeing the movie.

"We've not forgotten Kristen, Dad," David said, echoing his mother's words. "You had a very vivid dream brought on by the memory of your grief. I often dream of Kristen."

Jacob was not ready to acquiesce. "If it was just a dream, then why wouldn't she come into the house?"

David poured himself a fresh cup of coffee. "Dreams are funny things. They have their own kind of weird internal logic. Maybe the dream was saying that it is time for you to close the door on such sad memories and to remember Kristen as the bright and shining star that she truly was."

His mother smiled broadly in relief, as if hearing the correct answer to a perplexing riddle.

His father grunted and narrowed his eyes. "Now that I've had time to think more about it all, I'm truly afraid that it might really have been a demon disguised as Kristen," he said, offering his own explanation of his actions. "You two can sit there all day long and tell me it was just a dream, but I know better. I know that it really happened. Last night, a cruel demon took Kristen's form to deceive me and cause me pain. It really happened. It was not just some damn dream!"

His mother was rubbing her hands together anxiously, a nervous trait that David had observed since childhood. "That is such a terrible thing to say, Jacob! Our beautiful Kristen a demon? Shame on you! That was a terrible dream to have."

"No, no, don't you see," he tried to explain, clearly growing very impatient, "it wasn't a dream. It was a counterfeit Kristen that came knocking at our door to torment me. How often does the Bible warn us about spiritual counterfeits? And what is more, the demon that took Kristen's form told me that we would soon hear some news about her disappearance."

Carol shook her head in admonition. "Perhaps it was an angel in Kristen's form, not a demon. Oh, my Lord, to know at last what happened to our beautiful daughter. Dear Jesus, how wonderful that would be!"

Jacob brushed aside his wife's hopeful interpretation of his vision. "The spirit told me that what we will learn about Kristen will not be something that we will be pleased to hear."

"Any news after all these years would be welcome," David argued. "And I agree with Mom. You can't be certain that this apparition was evil."

His father snorted derisively. "That's right, isn't it? You've always believed in things that go bump in the night. Dear Lord deliver us, you even write stories about them."

It was nearly noon when David left his parents' home. He felt that his father would need to have some time to get over his nightmare about Kristen. There was nothing else that he could say or do to help at this point. At least his father was calmer now, drinking coffee with his mother.

David had barely driven a block into town when he saw the bright red flashing light in his rearview mirror. He breathed a sigh of relief when he saw that it was Sheriff Bill Nelson behind him. The two of them had been close friends since second grade. Bill probably wanted to remind him that he had promised to help him write an article that he wanted to submit to a detective magazine.

Bill got out and walked to his car, indicating that David should roll down his window. He was a tall man with just a trace of paunch betraying the fact that he, like David, was now in his fullsome forties. "Davy, gotta talk to you. Wanted to talk to you first . . . before I talked to your parents."

David shifted uncomfortably in his seat. "What's wrong?"

Bill opened the door on the passenger side and slid in beside him. They sat for a few uncomfortable moments in silence, then at last, Bill cleared his throat and spoke slowly, as if testing each word. "David, we found your sister. . . . I mean, we found Kristen's remains."

David felt as if his car had suddenly been tilted at a strange, disorienting angle. He thought of his father's eerie dream about Kristen. Had he experienced some kind of precognitive vision about the discovery of Kristen's remains that cloaked itself in the dream imagery of a lost daughter announcing her return home?

"Where did you find them . . . her remains?" After all these years, for God's sake! *Where?*

Bill swallowed hard, as if the words were painful to speak. "You know that there have been unusually heavy rains this spring. Some say that it's the heaviest rainfall in seventy years or more. Anyway, you know the big bend the Muskrat River makes at the old Swenson place? Well, the heavy rains made an even wider channel and exposed just the very top of a cave. About a week ago, some college boys spotted it and decided to go exploring. They found a big room inside the main part of the cave with . . . a skeleton."

"And you think it is . . . Kristen's . . . skeleton?" David was unable to prevent his body from trembling as he asked the question.

"We found her silver ankle bracelet on one of the leg bones," the sheriff told him. "I wouldn't let anyone release any information until I was damn certain. Kristen's dental records were still in the files at the office, so I sent them to the forensic boys at the state lab. They said it was Kristen without a doubt."

David felt tears well in his eyes. "Dear God. After all these years."

"I wanted to be damn sure before I talked to you and your parents," the sheriff said. "My God, you've had grief for nearly thirty years. From what the crime lab boys can piece together, some one must have grabbed her in town and . . . murdered her . . . and disposed of her body in that cave. Whoever it was, there surely are no clues remaining at this late date. We'll probably never know who did this terrible thing. But now, at least, for whatever consolation it will bring you and your folks, you finally know what happened to Kristen."

David felt the tears stinging his eyes. "She's come home at last."

Preparing for Unexpected Visitors from Shadow World

While none of us can completely prepare ourselves for an experience such as the one that the Christianson family underwent, we can examine it carefully and derive certain discussion points that might serve to prepare us for an unexpected visitor from Shadow World.

Some people with whom I have shared the Christianson's experience have been extremely critical of Jacob's decision that, in the final analysis, the entity that appeared at his doorstep was not truly his daughter, but a demon assuming her form to torment him. While the image of Kristen may truly have been that of her spirit preparing her family for the announcement of the discovery of her body after so many years, when we review the number of Spirit Mimics and Spirit Parasites that have deceived thousands, if not millions, of men and women down through the ages, we must conclude that Jacob did not react inappropriately.

Of course, one can also argue that it could have been a benevolent spirit masquerading as Kristen in order to begin the conditioning process that would at last bring closure to a family that has suffered for so long the unsettled grief of not knowing the fate of their beloved daughter and sister.

In dealing with the awareness that the denizens of Shadow World are out there just beyond the flimsy borders of our three-dimensional reality, it is best always to expect the unexpected and to prepare to encounter it. And one must not assume that all visitations by ethereal entities will be negative. Certainly many of the experiences that have been shared in this book have been positive, inspirational, and revelatory.

Clarisa Bernhardt and the Crossover Club

Psychic-sensitive Clarisa Bernhardt has been a good friend for many years. A few years ago, she told Sherry and me about the "Crossover Club" of spirits with whom she was working as a medium.

"In 1982, two years after the death of Mae West, who was extremely psychic, I was asked to serve as the medium at a séance that was held in the lounge of Hollywood's Ravenwood Apartments, where Mae had lived for nearly fifty years," Clarisa told us.

"Immediately I could feel a sense of joy coming from Mae's vibration," Clarisa continued. "She doesn't like the term *séance*, though; she prefers to say, 'interdimensional communication.' I think the most important thing that came out of the meeting was Mae telling us about the Crossover Club, a group of spirits who help new entities to adjust to life in that new dimension. She told us that she would soon be qualified to assist and to greet some of those who will be coming to the Other Side."

The information about the Crossover Club was of great benefit to a medium such as Clarisa, but the other sitters were more interested in seeking specific references to Mae West's life to convince them that they were, in fact, communicating with the late actress's spirit.

"Several of Mae's closest friends were there," Clarisa said, "and I was able to channel information that convinced them that her spirit essence was truly there. I received a communication about a problem with Mae's leg, that she had broken an ankle back in the 1940s but that no one else had known about it. Mae's spirit also referred to some inspirational writings of hers that she now felt might be helpful to others. She said that she had written ten to fifteen sheets on onionskin paper and placed them in a thin brown cover. A friend of hers confirmed that such papers did exist."

When Clarisa told the sitters in the spirit circle that Mae was expressing concern about a ring that had been lost, a friend of the actress immediately recognized the incident to which the spirit made reference. "He stated that only Mae and he knew about the lost ring."

Clarisa's Tips for Making the Supernatural Natural

Since that session in 1982, Clarisa Bernhardt has assisted many spirits to make their adjustment to the Other Side. "It is so important that we all keep our spiritual house in order," she said. "There are so many people who are unprepared to make their transition to a higher dimension. Part of my work—and that of the spiritual Crossover Club—is to encourage these confused entities to move on, to leave the earthplane, and to walk into the Light."

Clarissa advises people not to panic if they see a ghost. "Too many individuals panic and think the appearance of an apparition is beyond their reasoning. I tell them to follow my commonsense rules to handle the supernatural in a natural way."

DON'T SHOW FEAR. Psychic experiences and the appearances of spirits are normal facets of life and are far more common than many people realize. Some individuals have never taken the time to develop their spiritual abilities and exhibit fear when they encounter entities from the Other Side. Don't express fear unless you have a good reason to do so.

DON'T IGNORE YOUR PSYCHIC ENCOUNTERS. If the spirit of a deceased loved one should manifest before you, don't brush it off as an hallucination. Stop, look, listen, feel what the entity may be trying to tell you. There may be some unresolved issue in your life that needs to be addressed. Or, for example, if it should be the spirit of your mother, she may simply be telling you that she knows that you are thinking of her and she is showing you that she is thinking of you.

DON'T TAKE ALL SPIRIT OR PSYCHIC MESSAGES LITERALLY. Many spirit communications are symbolic. If you should experience a dream or a vision in which someone you know is about to die, you should not pick up the telephone and upset that person with what you believe to be a premonition. You may only have been given a sign that you should be paying more attention to that individual so your relationship doesn't "die." Or the vision of that person's death may represent him or her undergoing a rebirth, developing a new and more positive attitude toward life, or changing an occupation or profession.

COMBINE PSYCHIC IMPRESSIONS WITH COMMON SENSE. Be cautious of spirit advice concerning investments. If your uncle Joe wasn't a financial wizard in life, then chances are the death experience did not transform him into a Wall Street genius. You may, indeed, receive a valid impression or an accurate spirit message concerning your financial betterment. Just be certain that the intuitive hunch correlates with the hard facts that you can learn about the area of the investment.

BE JUDICIOUS IN DISCUSSING YOUR EXPERIENCES WITH OTHERS. It is unwise to share your spirit communications and psychic impressions with those who are skeptical or who hold religious views that frown upon such spiritual experiences. To receive a negative response to your interaction with the Other Side may cause you to block further important communications and lessons.

LEARN TO DEVELOP YOUR PARANORMAL ABILITIES. One good way of demonstrating the validity of your experiences is to write them down immediately. Since so many communications, symbolical and literal, occur in the dream state, keep a pen and tablet or a tape recorder beside your bed to record your dreams the moment you awake. If you have received a true prediction, it should come true within about three weeks.

Develop the ability to listen and to heed your subconscious, and you will encourage additional experiences and communications. As with any talent or ability, the more you use your psychic sense, the more it will grow and become a part of your everyday life.

Resisting Negative Spirits from Shadow World

Within Shadow World there exist some spirits that are bewildered, uncertain as to what occurred to them when death came. Others are still attached to people or places in our dimension of reality, and they wish to return to our material existence.

Those entities in the darkest regions of Shadow World are often filled with anger at finding themselves in a bleak and hostile domain of their own making. They try in every way to affect and to influence the minds and lives of all those living persons who will receive them. They wish to possess the living so that they might escape the hell of their own creation. It is such entities as these who are referred to as "demons" or "devils" from hell.

Whenever men and women lose control of their minds and their bodies through immoderate use of alcohol or drugs they recklessly open themselves to contact with these chaotic entities.

Whenever men and women choose to go about their daily activities emanating low-level vibrations of hate, jealousy, greed, or revenge, they make themselves vulnerable to contact with entities from the most chaotic regions of Shadow World.

Brad Steiger

Surrounding Yourself with a Positive Energy Field

If you should sense the presence of negative entities in your environment, practice this exercise.

Immediately visualize yourself slamming a door between you and the negative presence.

Next, visualize a golden energy of light moving upward from the bottoms of your feet to the top of your head. See it moving over your legs, your hips, your chest, your neck, right up to the top of your head. Then see the energy cascading down around you in sparks of golden light, as if you are being enveloped by the shimmering, sparkling outpouring of a roman candle.

Impress upon your consciousness that those "sparks" of golden light represent a new, positive energy field that surrounds you and forms a vital protective shield against all discordant and negative entities.

Visualize the Golden Light of Protection

If you have sensed an unseen presence that has left you feeling frightened and alone, immediately visualize the Golden Light of Protection forming itself around you. Calm yourself by saying, as you inhale, "*I am.*" On the outbreath, say, "*relaxed.*" Repeat this process a number of times until you feel yourself becoming calmer and more centered.

"I am," asserts your sovereignty and your uniqueness as an individual entity. "Relaxed" positively af-

258

firms your calm condition and establishes that you are in control of the situation.

Now visualize the image of a holy figure you hold in high esteem. See that holy figure taking your hand and standing beside you. Visualize the image of some person whom you love and trust completely. See that person taking your other hand and standing beside you. Feel strength, born of love, swell within your breast.

Know and understand that your Golden Light of Protection and the love of your friend and the holy figure have built an unpenetrable barrier between you and the negative unseen entities.

A Prayer of Protection from Negative Entities

Some individuals prefer uttering a prayer of protection as an immediate response to the presence of a seen or unseen negative entity. Many find the following prayer effective in such situations:

> O beloved [say here the name of your guide or holy figure] Light Being, send your protective light energies around me at once.
>
> Erect a shield of love and light about me that is invincible, all powerful, and unable to be penetrated by any evil force.
>
> Keep me totally protected from all things that are not of the Light or of God.
>
> Keep me immune from all negative and hostile beings. Banish at once the spirit that I see [feel] before me!

A Prayer for Renewed Strength and Energy

Many people who have encountered entities from Shadow World have suddenly felt themselves feeling drained of energy. If you should sense or perceive a negative entity in your environment and experience a sudden energy drain, say the following prayer.

> *Beloved Light Being [or the name of a holy figure or your angelic guide] fill me with your great strength.*
> *Charge me with your light and your love.*
> *Rejuvenate each of my vital body functions with strength and energy.*
> *Empower me with your might.*
> *Keep me now and always sensitive to your guidance and your direction.*

Cleansing Your Home of Negative Entities from Shadow World

Many great master teachers have declared the violet light ray from the Source-of-All-That-Is as constituting the highest vibratory level. Here is a ritual that many have used on a daily basis until their home feels purged of negative energy.

Call for the violet light and ask that your angelic/spirit guide connect you to the highest vibration of the Great Mystery, the Source of All that Is. Visualize the violet light moving over you in a wave of warmth. See it touching every part of your body (and the bodies of others if any are present). Feel it interacting with your spirit (and the spirits of all others who are present).

Say aloud to your guide:

Beloved _____ , assist me in calling upon the highest of energies from the Great Mystery. Provoke the law of harmony for myself [and for any others with you] and for all of us of mortal clay who have found ourselves in a dark place of shadows that resists the Light. Permit the violet light of transformation to move around and through this place of dwelling.

Allow the transforming energy to purify and to elevate all negative energies, all improper memories, all entities of evil purpose, all spirits who delight in wrongdoing, all vibrations that encourage impure desires.

Allow the transforming energy to replace all darkness with light. Remove all chaotic energies and replace them with the purest of energies, the power of love, and the glory of all good and benevolent spirits.

O _____ , bless us with light and so that we go forth on this new day of cleansing rejuvenated with perfect health, joy, illumination, and wisdom. Amen!

Within the borders of Shadow World there are those entities who seek to raise themselves to a higher dimension by keeping humankind low. These beings will seek always to possess the bodies and minds of humans and cause men and women to commit negative acts that poison the spirit. The most important thing to them seems to keep humankind on a lower, physical, animal-level so that they will always have an earthly kingdom in which to materialize and humans to subjugate.

While these negative beings consider themselves the Lords of the Earth, they are jealous of humankind's potential to rise to a dimension that is their birthright due to their cosmic heritage. There are many canyons, valleys, and hidden places in Shadow World, but the most chaotic regions within its borders can exist only if the Spirit Parasites can manage to keep large numbers of humankind debased and enslaved.

As I said in the beginning of this book, Shadow World exists all around us, a dark dimension that is sometimes frightening and always deserving of very cautious exploration. It is my earnest hope that I have provided some important guidelines that will prevent readers from becoming engulfed in a very real spiritual quagmire that they might not previously have been aware even existed.

Years ago, I used to close my lectures with a reading of my creed, my statement of belief. I would like to do that now, leaving each of you with something personal from me.

I believe that there is a Supreme Being, Timeless and Universal, to whom all men and women may reach out and receive strength.

I believe that the birth of all religions lies in the mystical experience of the individual and that all theologies and dogmas are but secondary growths superimposed.

I believe humankind is part of a larger community of intelligences, a complex hierarchy of powers and principalities, a potentially rich kingdom of interrelated species, both physical and nonphysical. Among these intelligences are multidimensional beings who care about our spiritual evolution.

I believe that humankind's one truly essential factor is its spirituality. The artificial concepts to which we have given the designation of sciences are no truer than dreams, visions, and inspirations. The quest for absolute proof or objective truth may always be meaningless and unattainable when it seeks to define and limit our Soul, which I believe is eternal, evolving higher in spiritual vibrations, seeking to return to the Source from whence it came.

I believe that technology plays a far smaller role in the lives of nations than the spirit, for the essence of humankind is its intellect and its Soul. Machines, associations, political parties, and trade balances are but transitory realities that must ultimately wither, decay, and come to nothing. The only lasting truths are Soul, imagination, and inspiration.

I believe that each man and woman, in moments of quiet meditation and prayer, may learn to enter the silence, enrich the Soul, and achieve a spiritual linkup with the blessed Harmony that governs the Universe.

SIGNET

__Brad Steiger and Sherry Hansen Steiger__

❏ CHILDREN OF THE LIGHT

0-451-18533-1/$4.99

❏ HEAVEN IS OUR HOME

0-451-19777-1/$5.99

❏ MOTHER MARY SPEAKS TO US

0-451-18804-7/$5.99

__Brad Steiger__

❏ GUARDIAN ANGELS AND SPIRIT GUIDES

0-451-19544-2/$5.99

❏ HE WALKS WITH ME

0-451-19213-3/$5.99

❏ ONE WITH THE LIGHT

0-451-18415-7/$4.99

❏ RETURNING FROM THE LIGHT

0-451-18623-0/$5.99

Prices slightly higher in Canada

Payable in U.S. funds only. No cash/COD accepted. Postage & handling: U.S./CAN. $2.75 for one book, $1.00 for each additional, not to exceed $6.75; Int'l $5.00 for one book, $1.00 each addition-al. We accept Visa, Amex, MC ($10.00 min.), checks ($15.00 fee for returned checks) and money orders. Call 800-788-6262 or 201-933-9292, fax 201-896-8569; refer to ad # STGR (1/00)

| Penguin Putnam Inc.
P.O. Box 12289, Dept. B
Newark, NJ 07101-5289
Please allow 4-6 weeks for delivery.
Foreign and Canadian delivery 6-8 weeks. | Bill my: ❏ Visa ❏ MasterCard ❏ Amex _____(expires)
Card# _____
Signature _____ |

Bill to:

Name _____.

Address _____ City _____

State/ZIP _____ Daytime Phone # _____

Ship to:

Name _____ Book Total $ _____

Address _____ Applicable Sales Tax $ _____

City _____ Postage & Handling $ _____

State/ZIP _____ Total Amount Due $ _____

This offer subject to change without notice.